OUT OF INDIA

OUT OF INDIA

A Raj Childhood

Michael Foss

MICHAEL O'MARA BOOKS LIMITED

First published in Great Britain in 2001 by
Michael O'Mara Books Limited
9 Lion Yard
Tremadoc Road
London SW4 7NQ

A CIP catalogue record for this book is available from the British
Library

ISBN 1-85479-806-5

1 3 5 7 9 10 8 6 4 2

Designed and typeset by SX Composing DTP, Rayleigh, Essex
Printed and bound in Great Britain by
Creative Print and Design (Wales), Ebbw Vale, Gwent

Contents

In the recovery of these events I thank my brother for the use of his memory, though the errors and misinterpretations are my own.

MICHAEL FOSS
March 2001

Prologue

WHAT HAVE I LEARNT?

Empty Tents

SOME TIME AGO I saw a picture on the back page of one of our national newspapers. It was a photo that had nothing to do with news or comment but was an artistic image indicating, I suppose, the respectable culture of the paper. The picture showed flooded land in India towards the end of the monsoon season, when the rising waters form temporary *jheels* or shallow lakes in the long hot flats of the plain and give to a land of too much desolation and dust the momentary charm of lakes and islands. Some water buffaloes were wallowing in this unexpected playground, their glistening black backs and the large sweep of their horns standing out just above the level of the water. A thin, barefoot boy in shorts and a loose cotton shirt was leaping from the back of one buffalo to another. The camera had caught him in mid-air, in an act of the utmost grace and agility. It was a picture of pure joy.

As I looked at it I thought I had never seen such a representation of an ideal childhood, a life so in tune with a particular place and time.

The boy in the photo was some ten or eleven years old, about the age that I was when I left India.

★

I hardly knew my father when I was young, since by profession he was a soldier and naturally had serious business to attend to in the early years of my life. Later perhaps I no longer wished to know him too well. I had never formed the habit of him and then it was too easy to drift away. Wartime separation, then boarding school, holidays apart from my parents abroad, a home quickly abandoned for a student apprenticeship, and then a flight to new lessons of the world and more hopeful skies – what chance did I have to overcome the shyness that crippled both of us, and the mutual suspicion of fathers and sons? When he died, an old man gasping from emphysema, trying to find bearings amid the scrabbled memories of Alzheimer's disease, there was, after the small griefs of the leave-taking, if not nothing, at least very little. I wondered at my . . . what? Unfilial coldness? Lack of charity? An impediment of the heart? He left me no keepsakes; but his watch, which remained unclaimed, came into my possession. In a similar casual manner, as if dropped behind in the fitful passage to quite another destiny, I found in my hands a large photograph album. I have been going through this album recently, again and again, trying to find the true tracks of early wanderings half-remembered, half-understood.

The photos dated from a period shortly before the First World War, pictures of an Anglo-Indian world ten to fifteen years before my father came to know it. The photos were large prints, the work of a professional photographer whom I assume to have been an Englishman. Large compositions, at that time, demanded some technical dexterity, and portraiture of the Raj also required tact and a proper sense of the rightness of things. The task was not lightly entrusted to Indians. So I imagine the photographer, a civilian tradesman deferential perhaps in the presence of so much military brass, in Norfolk jacket and plus-fours, his head ducking in and out from beneath the green baize cloth that covered the bellows of the box camera. He was in any case a competent man. His pictures came out clear and sharp and well-composed, many in the sepia tint that always lends nostalgia to the most ordinary of everyday events.

Most of the photos were of regimental groups and places, or views of Indian towns and landscapes, particularly on the mountainous north-western borders fronting onto Afghanistan. There were confident group portraits of the English officers and the Indian subadars and jemadars of the 57th Frontier Force. This was the regiment known as Wilde's Rifles, which my father later joined. There were views of the town and the hills and the Army Signalling Station at Kasauli, in the foothills of the Himalayas. There were views of Peshawar and the bleak eroded mountains and the little lonely hill stations beyond, at the limit of safety, in the harsh wilderness that the regiments of the Indian Army Frontier Force were supposed to keep secure for civilization against the Pathans of the hills, those inveterate brigands and disturbers of all colonial peace. Then there were flat vistas of the Indus plain, an expanse so vast and empty that it was in its own way as cheerless and intimidating as the mountains themselves. And lastly, in a big group, there were numerous photographs of the great Indian durbar that took place in Delhi in 1911.

It seems to me that some huge matters were implicit in those images. A powerful moment in history, if only I could catch it. Again and again I turn over the pages of these photos, drawn to the scenes of that durbar.

From all over British India the soldiers and the administrators of the Raj had collected to do honour to the King-Emperor (such a title for that middle-aged gent in a tight coat, with his bug-eyed Hanoverian stare hardly humanized by a bluff sailor's beard!). The photographer had taken many pictures by day and by night, of the temporary military encampments around Delhi. By day, ranks of empty army tents, squared-off in the straight lines beloved of the military mind, were strung out amid the yellowing grass, the scrub and the low trees on the edge of the Old City of Delhi. It looked as if the city was encompassed by the lines of an invading army. An enemy was penned within. By night, under the flare of petroleum lamps, the pale forms of the tents looked ghostly and alien, a sublunary world full of menace.

Inside this ring of tents a Moghul gate to the Old City, ablaze with floodlight, was hung with a giant picture of George V and carried across the main arch, in very large English letters, the legend LONG LIVE THE KING-EMPEROR. I wondered at the effrontery of this message, smack in the face of a teeming oriental city that spoke many local languages but where only the clerks and the well-heeled could have read English. The message, quite obviously, was one of self-satisfaction directed elsewhere than at the Indian population.

On the field of the durbar a square dais with many slender columns was topped by a gilded onion-dome, under which the King-Emperor was seated. The effect was not fortunate. Here East and West jostled, and the Brighton Pavilion came to mind rather than the court of Akbar. At the foot of the dais Indian soldiers in dark uniforms and white topees guarded a compound marked off by a velvet rope. Indian princes and high officials in their best ceremonial robes looked on from a small but sufficient distance. The impression was of a sunny day at a Royal Ascot race-meeting. Several of the high-ranking men – I could see no women in this enclosure – were sheltering from the sun under black umbrellas more often seen in a London winter. Around the important people was an empty space. Then the mass of spectators sat in a broad circle under an awning striped like circus canvas. All these spectators were Europeans, the men in uniforms as spick and span as braid, polish and brass could make them, and the women in iridescent silks and feathers looking as flighty as a flock of Himalayan pheasants.

This durbar of 1911 was the last great imperial occasion in India. The last inflation of the bubble before the pricking of nationalism caused that confident gas to leak rapidly away. The durbar spoke clearly and without embarrassment of old rapine, old strength, old moral blindness. But the Delhi it was aimed at, the witness of the *tamasha*, was no longer the old seat of ancient empire, the Moghul city so knocked about in the mutiny siege of 1857. It was now a place handed back to the puzzle and mess of ordinary life. It had become a ramshackle city where the ever-growing native popu-lation – Hindus and Muslims mixed and stirred among members of all the peoples of northern India – spilled out into a huge cock-crowing, donkey-braying, cattle-lowing caravanserai down on the stony bank of the Yamuna river. A place of shanties, godowns and befouled lanes made alive by the necessity and energy of poverty. That was the real Delhi. Durbar Delhi was little more than a theatrical back-drop, painted for the delusion of England. It was a stage-set that pretended to imitate the grandeur of the Potsdam of Frederick the Great or even the Versailles of the Sun King.

The durbar and its aftermath, which saw the New Delhi of the British Raj arise under the showy architectural hand of Edwin Lutyens, was England dreaming. It was too late for dreams. Sick of the malady of empire, the nationalist movement was beginning to kick India awake.

★

Looking back at the world of these photos I do not know whether

I belonged to the betrayers or the betrayed. Have I turned in disgust from the tomfoolery of this transposed England, so fatefully placed under the wide kite-wheeling skies, where vultures rooted in dead bodies on the tops of the Towers of Silence? Have I, in a cricketing phrase beloved of British-educated Indians, 'let the side down'?

Or have I been restrained, by timidity or training or perhaps some disability inherent in imperial genes, from finding a worthwhile path in that great, muddled, dangerous, dazzling maze into which I had been born?

★

I was born in the British Military Hospital of one of those little northern hill stations, at Murree, where the families of the Raj took refuge each year from the summer heat of Rawalpindi. A couple of years before the Second World War, I was hastened into the langorous after-midnight hours of a July night by an Australian army doctor anxious not to miss the Bombay boat booked for his leave. For him, as for most of us, India, whatever it was, did not count as home. There was always a boat out that one could not afford to miss.

Just before the start of the war I too was on a boat, taken into exile to a land called England, reputed to be *my* home.

PART I

WAR GAMES

ONE

A Child's View of
the Ocean

ONCE MORE, WE were on a ship, all our family together, leaving Glasgow to return to India.

When the inscrutable military had brought us back from India, despite the alarms of Munich and an impending war, my father had been assigned to a 'course' in Northern Ireland. The aim of this course remained mysterious to him. He, a sunburnt soldier of a dry and withered Indian frontier, was sent under weepy skies to the foggy green fields around Belfast to mould territorials whose destiny still tottered between appeasement and Hitler. Trained to try to read the runes of a lawless wilderness, where bloodlust, treachery and a cheerful aptitude for guerrilla warfare had made life hot for all regular forces with a pretension to modernity and efficiency, from Alexander the Great to Emperor Babur and then onward to the Indian Army of the Raj, my father now found that the nice judgement demanded of him was to distinguish carefully between Paddy and Prod.

In an unguarded moment in the territorial Officers' Mess he had admitted that he was married to a southern Irish Catholic. In consternation, a friendly hand had led him outside. 'For goodness' sake, man,' the local had whispered, 'if you value your health in these parts, *never* admit to have anything to do with Catholics.' The instruction was not so much military as a lesson for life. But valuable though it was my father did not feel that it warranted a journey from India. Even after the declaration of war, when my father was impatient to get back to his regiment and anxious also to take his wife and two very young boys away from the whistle of bombs and the stringency of rationing, he was forced to study for a while longer the punctilio of religious difference ground out in sweat and blood over some two hundred and fifty years of extreme prejudice.

'Perhaps,' my father told me later, at the start of more recent Irish troubles, 'it was not so very different from the world of the Frontier.'

In the summer of 1940 he received orders to return with his family to India.

★

Today, when I think of the sea, it holds no particular terrors. Everyone of sense respects the sea, that latent danger, the shifts and swell of the water that suggest nothing so much as the bunching of titanic shoulders. Storms are always fearful, and the thought of drowning is a door I would not open, for that nether world is dark and ominous beyond conjecture. Yet I have good reasons to fear the sea.

★

Out of nowhere, I am standing on a deck. I am holding a hand and I can feel the edges of a precious stone set in a ring. I am not apprehensive. It is cold but not excessively so – late September chill – and I am dressed in warm stuff as for some trek or adventure, though what that could be in the depth of the night I have no idea. A long way below I can make out the black mat of the sea. It is heavy and stirs easily with a calm procession of small swells. The moon looks enormous in cloudless skies, making everything sharp and clear.

It is saying: Now, this is a moment not to be missed.

At a distance all around are friendly quiet shapes, familiar ships very like our own as if a hand might casually pluck them from the bath at bedtime. Engines have stopped and I hear only the light slap of the sea at the water line. There is no song of the wind in the rigging, and the canvas covers on the lifeboats are as taut as a drum. I stand among adults as stiff as lead soldiers, as silent as sleep.

All this is the grammar of toytown, formal and static and emptied of emotion, so that even a child of three could begin to understand it.

Suddenly, in my memory, the scene has become animated with meaning and consequence, and I now realize that for the first time I was not only hearing but also recording the strange demotic language of life.

We had been brought to the deck, where we had been standing for some time, by dull thuds suffusing up from below the surface of the sea. What did they mean, those slow heavy bubbles of doubt and unease bursting out from unseen monsters? The sailors amongst us on the crowded decks knew those signs well enough. Most of the passengers guessed but hoped helplessly that this fate might pass them by. They were landlubbers, after all, without any commitment to the realm of the sea. From time to time, on a neighbouring ship that seemed uncomfortably near, a spurt of flame would flare and die, a match lit and extinguished with its work smartly done. Then one of the ships dotted around us would gradually tip and with a sad grace slip slowly away.

For us, what course would the officers of the night pick between hope and despondency? After an age of looking, the naval mind was made up. Orders were barked along the deck, petty-officers and ratings began to muster their crews. Seamen sprang to work on the lifeboats and on the lockers that held the lifebuoys and lifejackets, cutting through lashings, hammering padlocks from the hasps, ripping away canvas, clearing davits, working not frantically but with enough clumsy urgency to suggest some slow but unstoppable calamity. Frustration squeezed the labouring bodies like a vice, as men lunged at tangled and fouled ropes, or were balked by corroded metal and layers of gummed-up paintwork. Lungs short of air blurted out in gasps: 'Christ almighty, these bloody ropes!' 'Kick the bastard, get it moving, damn you!' 'Whoa, get a grip there, *don't* let it swing!' Then curses, oaths, dark-faced mutterings, pungent and repetitious, bewailing fate, maligning all the gods for this terrifying mess of life – the usual story.

Ropes stiffened by age and salt water resisted muscle power. Fingers were torn and bleeding. An axe was called for, then a line parted with a deadly twang and a shriek from a rusted pulley. Lifeboats partly cleared jerked in their davits, swinging unevenly, heeled at mad angles. The crowd on the decks stood by, frowning with worry and concentration. Young men volunteered to help but were turned back with brusque unfriendly shakes of the head. The seamen had enough to contend with already. Panic, if it were panic, was beginning to lap at the common expectation of the onlookers, like the damp creeping through the thrown-on slippers of the passengers, who now had to pull back from the rails at which sailors were bumping and cursing.

But no, it wasn't panic. The danger was not yet so extreme. We were facing adversity, not annihilation, and we were gathering ourselves for another display of fortitude. This was the year of Dunkirk, and the summer's evacuation from the beaches was strong in the memory. Our people knew what was expected of them. We acted now under the compulsion of our history and psychology. Was it any the less heroic to do so?

So this unspoken mass-history seemed to make even small children stoical. Did we feel it in our bones, my brother and I, a sort of perverse rectitude, a good behaviour far beyond our years and quite alien to frightened children? There we stood quietly, in a quiet crowd, clutching our mother's hands. I could not see our tall father but no doubt he was in his proper place, for this was an orderly event. In any case I was small and hemmed in by legs. From my low level I had a view of naked ankles, bare feet thrust into slippers, gym-shoes, unlaced army boots, polished brogues, even court shoes with improbably giddy heels. Looking up a little I saw nightdresses with pretty frills peeping below the hem of bright dressing-gowns, striped pyjamas tucked into boot-tops, the jacket of a battle-dress buttoned over an evening shirt with a wing collar, a long scarf in school colours wound around an old woman's neck. Men were unshaven, with the smudged look of interrupted sleep; women patted unkempt hair, or hugged a winter coat tight above the slinky material of nightclothes. For us children, all this was neither comic nor monstrous. Caught by the sobriety of our surroundings, we thought it an unusual prelude leading to some unknown grown-up ritual. Some enactment, we felt with more interest than alarm, was about to begin.

The big moon radiated a calm light, clarifying even the smallest movement, making it look weighty and deliberate. We watched, holding a collective breath. At a distance, another ship was foundering. Then somewhere below our feet, in the bowel of our ship, there was a crump and a slight shudder. Then an intensified silence. An effervescent flurry of small bubbles popped out of the crack between the hull and the ocean, dancing in moonlight. The jolt shook the doubt from the face of the crowd. Now we knew for sure, the worst expectation was realized, but the knowledge gave a certain courage.

The fate of the ship was now decided, but the percussion below had led to no sudden appalling consequence and the discipline held along the decks. After a while there seemed to be a hardly perceptible tilt to the hull. Only the now furious action of the crew warned of the inevitable denouement.

A rush of feet, shouts of authority, flushed faces under naval caps waving blue sleeves circled with the rings of their rank. A young officer's voice choking on an embarrassing squeak. Sailors cutting into the crowd on the decks like handlers at a cattle-drive, rounding up nervous groups, heading off the lost or the maverick. Distortions bawled over the loudspeakers of the public address system, barely comprehensible – 'Calling Muster Station G', 'Officers' wives and dependent children', 'Starboard evacuees', 'Remember your lifeboat drill'. The whirr of electric motors, wire screaming off the drum, lifeboats plunging downwards and banging brutally into the water. People getting hastily into lifejackets, puffed as turkey-cocks, the bulging canvas of the jackets soiled by water-stains. Rope ladders flung over the rails, uncoiling like strange probosces. Bosun's chairs swinging out into space.

My father was gone. Sometime in the stir and haste of the moment he, with other adult males, had been led away. Was there some logic applied to quitting a ship that decreed the break-up of families? I could not understand this dividing of our paths. Now more than ever I needed that tall figure, that paterfamilias. I renewed my grip on my mother's hand. We – 'wives and dependent children' – were herded to a bay in the deck-rail where a bosun's chair hung out from a cantilevered steel beam. How did one connect that skimpy canvas contraption on the end of a rope with the necessity of escape and safety? Anxiety made my brother's face look strained and white in the moonlight, startlingly white, but he would not cry. My senior by a couple of years, he felt an elder's responsibility. He had a boil on his bottom. As for me, if only I remained clutching my mother's hand I was secure.

A lifeboat was bobbing below, too close under the hull to be seen from the deck. Oars splashed awkwardly in inexpert hands. Male voices rose from the lifeboat, unnaturally hearty, ringing with false confidence, contradictory voices used to command but well out of their element now. A woman climbed over the rail and set herself gingerly on a rope ladder, descending very carefully until only her fastidious wrinkled forehead was above the deck. A child was quickly tied into the bosun's chair and dropped from sight like a stone.

In the mild night the evacuation was going quickly and smoothly but the plates of the ship were groaning and the stern was beginning to hunker down like an exhausted dog.

'Hurry, for goodness' sake get a move on,' came a voice from below, 'or this damn boat is going to squat on us. Double up the kids in the canvas chair.'

Along the deck a fat little boy, bigger than my brother and just old enough to start to form some cloudy notion of the ultimate danger, had changed from subdued snivels to raucous hiccups of fright. My brother was being settled into the chair when an exasperated sailor, unnerved by these squalls, grabbed the fat kid and thrust him onto the lap of my much smaller brother. Then down they went, my brother's pinched face peeping from behind the enveloping suet of puppy fat. My mother and I followed, her arms tight about me.

The last passenger came unsteadily down the rope ladder and a voice cried, 'Leave off there, this boat's full now.' Oars were hovering above the surface of the sea and the lifeboat was kicked away from the scales of the rusty hull. Out from the shelter of the ship we sat on the swell, waiting for a signal from above that all was clear to pull away from the drowning ironwork of the stricken ship. On a bench in the lifeboat my brother and I crouched under the lee of my mother's body, her arms hugging around our shoulders. My brother looked at the plump brat still trying to ride his hiccups and whispered with tears in his own voice, 'He sat on me and burst my boiler.'

★

A brilliant night, out under the stars. Mythological wonders of gods and heroes were written on the palimpsest of the sky; I looked up with eyes new to this creation and felt instinctively the power of that divine writing that had suggested such a persuasive mystery to Sumerians, Babylonians, Egyptians, Chinese, Indians, Greeks,

Polynesians, even to those weird blue men tending the ancient boulders of Stonehenge. The cold nip of the night gave a polish to the air, making those lights of heaven sparkle. We were alone now. The ship had gone, a quiet demise, slipping almost unnoticed into the confraternity of the deep. We held position according to the wheeling arms of the Plough and the certainty of the Pole Star. Somewhere not far to the south was Donegal or the coast of Northern Ireland. If we pulled steadily towards the east Glasgow awaited us. The rowers put their backs into the oars. There was nothing else to do.

Men had ranged themselves along the wooden benches, two or three to each oar, depending on their age and strength. The lifeboat was heavy and clumsy with high sides, deliberately overbuilt to stand the punishment of the ocean, and it was not easy to row. The hands on the oars were willing but soft, inexperienced. The oars were long, heavy, with rough wooden handles. They struck the water at an awkward angle, and the knack of getting them in and out smoothly with a steady rhythm was hard to learn. After a while no one spoke. A bearded man vested in the authority of a navy-blue jacket with brass buttons took the tiller. Women and children were scattered on the benches towards the inside of the boat, fitting in wherever there was a space. The rowers had begun briskly but soon grew weary. Shoulders slumped, breath came thickly from open mouths, a dew of sweat dampened foreheads even in the night chill. Sore hands began to blister. The breeze was freshening, dragging frayed strips of cloud over the flying moon. When the moon was hidden, the oar-strokes no longer glittered in a spray of white foam but went in and out amid surly dark swirls.

Our little family group sat facing forward, cramped for space but glad to huddle together for warmth and security. My brother's back came within the ambit of one of the oarsman's swing. Every so often, on a hard pull, the end of the oar jerked into my brother's body. A creak of the oar-lock and then the blow – a painful time-keeping. It was not easy to shift position without disrupting the work of the boat, and my brother did not complain. He was older than I and felt his standing, particularly in the absence of our father. He would not acknowledge his bruises, and this was no time for the indulgence of tears. At first, I sat on my mother's lap, hugged against the rough stuff of her coat. In front of me I watched the prow circle against the starry sky. The long swell under the rising breeze was causing the lifeboat to yaw and pitch a little, a mild but unsteady motion.

The fusty smell of my mother's coat was in my nose. I felt constricted. I was gulping, I couldn't get enough air, a rising warmth pushed against a plug of soft matter in my throat. My eyes were out of kilter, the horizon was up-ending itself, faces shifted alarmingly. I needed more room. Seeing my condition my mother led me down the boat, stumbling over the ribs, to the clear space in the stern around the helmsman. On each side of him a little bench curved around the contour of the boat just below the gunwale. We sat on one of these benches, close to the helmsman, but I could not prevent the welling up of my young life inside me. Fright, cold, puzzlement, misery, ignorance, the loneliness of a small mite on the vast unfeeling breast of the sea, they all gripped me. I began to gasp. Now I knew where I was, raw and almost unlicked, and for the first time I sensed my human incapacity. My eyes were misted, my stomach churned and heaved.

Suddenly I leant forward and vomited accurately into the lap of the helmsman. He hardly flinched but kept tired eyes straining into the night.

★

Biological life is one thing. We date our being from conception or birth. But except in dreams or drugs what do we know of our infant days, our weaning, our first stumbles onto two legs, our shouts of naked emotion turning by degrees into speech? Full life – full self-awareness – starts with the first memory. I know that moment exactly. I confirmed it at the City of London Library at the Guildhall, searching through the shipping registers of Lloyd's of London. I read there what I already knew, that when reality caught me and opened my eyes to perception I was hand-in-hand with catastrophe and sudden violence:

Departed from the Clyde, on 19 September 1940, SS *City of Simla*, with 3000 tons of general cargo, 183 crew and 167 passengers. On 21 September, at 55′59″ North & 8′16″ West, torpedoed at 1.35 a.m. and sunk, with the loss of 1 crew and 2 passengers.

TWO

The Gate Closed

'LISTEN, CHILDREN,' SAID the voice, trying to be cheerful, 'who's going to be the first to see a ship?' It was a poor game but we took it up eagerly, glad, in our anxiety, to be diverted. The mind finds a narcotic in its own patterns of activity – in *this* preoccupation we swerve away from *that* fear. A clump of darkness, the shadow of a cloud, a moon-bright slick on a wave, one by one such queer shapes gave a fillip to our childish imagination. But no ship came. Then we grew weary and subsided into uneasy dozing, keeled over against adults, starting awake at the pitch of the boat or the ruffle of the wind.

At dawn, a watery sun peered blearily over the far hump of the ocean. For several hours we had been rowing through seas more cheerless than dangerous. The calm weather was holding. The unwieldy oars scratched along the water, ticking off the slow passage of time. In the lifeboat heads were drooping, on the edge of sleep or nodding vaguely to a dejected rhythm. So no one saw the pale flush of the day's first meagre light pick out the lines of a freighter far ahead steaming very slowly across our bows. Then the adults saw it and a low noise went around the boat, not jubilant or excited, but as if taking satisfaction in a favourable toss of the coin. How quickly it had been accepted, in this Britain of 1940, that an autumnal night in an open boat on the North Atlantic was merely the ill luck of war, to be expected and endured. For the time being the good citizen had abandoned the habitual cry of self- interest, the demand to be heard first and often. We were learning that there was a kind of peace in unaccustomed humility.

The rowers rested on their oars, craning awkward looks over the shoulder. They saw the freighter alter course and begin to grow bulky in their line of sight, huge and grey. Then they could afford to smile wearily and paddle a little, sagging on the benches, fatigue mixed with relief giving them a fatuous or spaced-out look.

The freighter had been tiptoeing carefully past the U-boats towards Glasgow. The radio had reported the sinkings in our convoy and so the freighter was not surprised to find lifeboats adrift on the night seas. The crew had already picked up other survivors and had weather eyes open for more boats in need of rescue. Now it was our turn. The big ship hove to, and we slopped about in the thick gloom of its hull. High above us, along the deck-rail, were rows of whitish faces, as dim as dinner plates in a dusty old-fashioned dresser. No one waved or shouted. In a minute or so a dark-faced lascar shook out a coil of rope and hurled it into the bow so that we could tie up and bring the lifeboat alongside the sloping gangway suspended against the side of the ship. We began a laborious disembarkation, a painful exit blotting out the memory of how smartly we had jumped for our lives into the boat. We had been wrung out by too much emotion. This was no more than a domestic event, a homecoming of weary travellers that required neither banners nor trumpets.

And in this flat atmosphere somehow it did not startle me that I should find my father waiting for us as we stepped from gangway to deck. What is a homecoming without the father of the house? His lifeboat had been picked up a good hour before us. I do not remember that he hugged us, but I think he gave my brother and myself a manly shake of our little hands.

But we were fretful and demanding, wanting some recognition of the magnitude of our childhood adventure. Grizzling, wiping tired eyes with the back of a sleeve, shivering not so much from cold but in the after-shock of sea and misery, we went moaning and complaining to a gaunt, functional lobby where we could rest under an old coat or blanket, prone on the floor or huddled in crooked shapes on one of the few armchairs.

We slept, ate hard biscuits and drank weak tea, then dozed again while the freighter headed for Glasgow. As we entered the docks at nightfall we kids were still fractious and bickering, making a grievance of our new safety, paying out for lost security with a litany of whines. Our mother was overwhelmed, as so often, and then exhausted to the point of tears. That she should have to endure this, after all that *she* had been through. She washed her hands of us, with resentful looks towards her husband, implying the need for a father's firm hand. The provocation of his family was as much as my father could bear at the best of times. He hoped to be above the sordid fray of family disputes. In India, there had always been an ayah to scoop us up out of the sahib's wrath, to feed us sweetmeats and a taste of *pan* in the servants' cubbyhole behind the kitchen.

'Now, boys,' he said reproachfully, 'you know better than to annoy your mother.'

He hoped that would be enough, but of course it hardly ever was, and he was reduced to the indignity of having to issue threats and smacks at random. It was sad the effort he had to make to knock us about, and I think we felt for him, for we redoubled our noise and not all the laments were for ourselves. We felt the suffering of our parents.

After all, what did our family have left? We stood in an ill-assorted jumble of clothes. Our trunks, our cases, all our household effects, a favourite teddy bear and the other inconsequential toys of childhood were even then settling into the silt of the North Atlantic. We had become refugees in our own land, a place to which we were barely connected, bearing odd garments like the stigma of our dispossession. My father, tall and slim and a bit of a dandy in his dress, had been given a flat-top cap in a cheerful tweed, the chummy sort of cap of beer-stained working-class pubs in the industrial north of England. We trudged out of the ship onto a raw dock surrounded by the spires of cranes. My brother and I were dragging our feet, trying to put our sullenness into words.

'What an awful hat,' said my brother gloomily, behind our father's back.

'Horrible,' I replied.

No one was paying attention. We plodded on through a battered perimeter gate to confront the city of Glasgow and the unknown land beyond. An elderly sentry with a .303 Lee-Enfield rifle from the time of the Great War carefully closed the gate after us.

★

'Whose bairns are these?' the old man said again, crinkling his eyes and squeezing a little rheumy water out at the corners.

The thin old lady with the ramrod-straight back looked up from polishing boots and replied sharply, 'Why, Tom, you know they're Fred's of course.' And she added with a severe glance towards the pale young woman sewing on the other side of the fire. 'And *she's* his wife.'

My grandmother would not mention my mother's name, if she could avoid it. My mother was Irish and 'Roman' while my grand-mother was a strict Wesleyan Methodist. My anxious mother, always so worried and unsure and willing to help, was classed among the ranks of the Scarlet Women.

My grandfather nodded peacefully, crumbling a biscuit into his cup of tea. Reassured once more as to the provenance of the little strangers who had burst so surprisingly into the tranquil life of his retirement, he continued to pass us titbits of broken biscuit under the cover of the heavy tablecloth, where my grandmother could not see it.

Soon after the sinking of the *City of Simla*, my father had been sent back to India by plane. But there was no longer any escape for families. Now ships were too dangerous, and planes too valuable for the brutalities of war to be used for the sake of families. By default, having nowhere else to go, we trailed out of Glasgow heading for my father's home village in Lincolnshire, most subterranean and glum of English counties.

We came to a brick cottage on a quiet road at the end of the village. The house was very small, a parlour at the front, a kitchen and scullery at the back with a cold-water tap and an eternal chill rising from the stone flags of the floor. In the corner a cupboard door led straight onto the stairs, bare deal planks in a dark enclosure of lath and plaster leading to the two little bedrooms above. There was no bathroom. A zinc tub hung under the lean-to outside the back door. On bath nights it was carried into the kitchen to be filled with scalding water from the big black kettle on the hob. The lavatory was in an outhouse at the bottom of the garden, a single seat above the ordure pit in a dusty wooden hut that doubled as a shed for storage of tools, garden implements, oddments and junk.

For us children this was a place of wonder. We squatted above the not unpleasant sweet-sour hum that came off the digestive rot below, amid spiders' webs and the desiccated corpses of flies, and the yellowing leaves of old newspapers, and rusted bicycle parts, and broken cloches jostling with dirt-encrusted flowerpots, and my grandfather' tools on the high oil-soaked shelves from where a hammer had fallen on the nose of my father in the midst of a youthful reverie. It broke the ridge of his nose and left him with a rather distinguished patrician bump.

The outhouse had no electricity. Daytime wonders became frights in the winter dark as we went unwillingly down the long brick path, comforted only by the feeble light of a kerosene lantern, to that insect- and vermin-haunted glory-hole. At night, it was a relief to jump into bed assured of the solidity of a massive china chamber-pot resting beneath the bedsprings.

The cottage was a tied dwelling attached to a job on the Londesborough agricultural estates where my grandfather had worked all his labouring life. As a lad he began as a groom in the stables, chasing watery suds with a broom around the horses' hoofs, raking the warm brown flanks with a curry-comb, polishing the brass and the leather tackle. He had progressed into the yellow livery of a servant, a smart young fellow on the lead horse or the whip hand on the high seat of the aristocratic carriage. The new century had phased out the horses and my grandfather withdrew from the stables with them, unable to get a grasp on the newfangled mechanicals of the motor cars that had replaced the horses. He became an ordinary estate worker – field-hand, woodsman, park-keeper, ornamental and kitchen gardener, seasonal beater on aristocratic shoots. Year after year the same round, following the tail of the weather – digging, planting, weeding, mowing, hedging, felling, leaf-burning; the same wet soil, wet grass, wet hay, wet leaves. He tied a loop of string round the trousers at ankle level and kept his balding head out of the sun. His eyes acquired a weather-wise squint. The work suited him.

In placid sequence he and his wife had four girls, country lasses with stout legs and broad bottoms and sensible views on life, bursting out of the tiny upstairs bedroom. Then twelve years after the last girl, and twenty after the birth of the eldest sister, came my father, a sickly runt and an afterthought from an almost exhausted womb. The advent of this late son, who had nearly done for his mother in childbirth and who was both delicate and clever, caused a softening of my grandmother's iron-clad heart. She unbent far enough to spoil him, and in this she was enthusiastically helped by the four robust sisters.

My grandfather left home matters in the hands of his capable wife and daughters. His only son grew into a bookish, bright lad, a scholarship winner at the local grammar school. He was completely devoid of a countryman's ways and interests. He never did know a robin's egg from a blackbird's. A maple looked the same as a sycamore. And digging was forbidden to one of such delicate health. To my father, fishing and hunting and shooting were murderous pursuits for the coarse-minded gentry and the slack-mouthed aristocracy. My grandmother forgave him all his idiosyncrasies and insisted on one thing only – a regular weekly attendance on Sunday in the Methodist chapel. My father went, but he angled it so that he was put in charge of the bellows on the little organ, which was operated from outside the building by a long handle through the wall. When a hymn was coming up the organist would call for wind by sharp raps on the wall. Squatting outside, my father put down his cigarette (he was a keen smoker from an early age) and his copy of Sexton Blake or Sherlock Holmes and started pumping the bellows.

My grandfather allowed himself some pride in the unusual and academic range of his son's activities. But he did not concern him-self with household affairs, among which education was included, and was content to remain puzzled though admiring. In the steady habit of his life he came from field or garden to the house, knocked the mud from his boots and laid them carefully just inside the back door, then went in stockinged feet across the polished gloss of the parlour floor to his usual chair on the right of the fireplace.

I remember him there in his old age, when his wits had begun to wander a little. He had trouble with his feet and hobbled in old carpet slippers with pieces cut out to ease his toes. Watching him take the weight off his feet with a sigh, I could not decide which was more kindly – the winking glow of the few coals in the fire, or his genial broad country face, scoured by so many changing seasons, topped by fringes of soft white hair. Settled in his chair he was ready to begin the solemn ritual of his pipe. He reamed out the black dottle, teased strands of tobacco from the block, and tamped the bowl with a stained thumb. Then taking a long paper spill from a holder on the mantel he would turn to one of us children. 'Now, young fellow –' he could never remember our names – 'here's a little job for you.' My brother or I would light the spill in the coals and with much care take the glowing paper to his gnarled hand. In a while he had the pipe drawing well. He closed his eyes in a modest bliss that temporarily wiped from the often confused terrain of his face the field-marks and etched scars of many thousand hard working days.

In his later years my grandfather did not have far to go to work. All along one side of his garden ran a high wall of solid brickwork. This wall continued far beyond my grandfather's small plot, enclosing in a wide embrace a Victorian mansion and its extensive grounds. All this belonged also to the Londesborough estate. An elegant reverend clergyman lived here. He was a churchman of the old Anglican school, a muscular Christian with a general licence to rectify social manners and keep a watch on the lower orders. He was perpetually busy in what he assumed to be God's terrestrial kingdom but with no particular responsibility other than to follow the strenuous life of the sporting parson. He had been a famous cricketer and had done notable things at the wicket for England. For this, the government of the day had granted him a Civil List pension. He lived in gentlemanly ease, well attended by servants, with my grandfather assigned to him as gardener and ground-keeper. In time there had arisen between the priest and my grandfather a dispute about land. The Reverend, with time and leisure to poke among certain ancient deeds, had concluded that he had a right to a large part of my grandfather's garden. The long thin plot of this garden was vital to the lean economy of my grandfather's household, and he made use of every inch of soil and space: the neat beds of green and root vegetables bordered by marigolds; the potato patch and the marrows under the hedge; the raspberry canes tied up with green twine; the bushes of red and black currants; the trimmed fruit trees, a big Bramley and a nondescript eater with a pinkish flesh; and lastly, the provider of good garden muck, the pig in its little sty, fattening on the kitchen swill, waiting for the autumnal slaughter and the consequent gifts of ham and bacon and sausages and chitterlings. In the long evenings and at weekends my grandfather gave his garden serious and professional attention. For him this was no light recreation. The produce that came out of it was not something extra but was essential to the well-being of his family.

When he considered the poverty of his neighbour, the clergyman thought that those needs, real though they were, accounted for little against his own property rights. The exaltation of his own privilege, living as he did on the fat plenty of an unearned pension, should not be lessened even out of Christian charity, for that put in question the whole mystical arrangement of a propertied hierarchy. After all, the Reverend looked on himself as a kindly man, and his gardener should have confidence in that. He should know that the Reverend merely acted out of principle.

Mildly, my grandfather protested against the land-grab in his garden. But he willingly submitted himself to the obscure and almost secret decisions of his betters. He rested his case, not on the law or advocacy, but on whatever turn of mind the gentry might take that day. Even if he had had the means (which of course he didn't), he would not go to law. So in some unimaginable court of social usage, where poor people had no representation and no appeal, a verdict was handed down, most surprisingly, in my grandfather's favour. Though he did not know how it happened, he was content. Whatever way the judgement had gone he would still have stepped from the path and pulled the cap from his head for the Reverend whenever they met, and my grandmother would have bobbed her rigid back in something that might just have been taken for a curtsy.

★

On the other side of the road from the cottage, behind a verge of uncut grass and a tangle of bushes, ran a little stream. The water there, in that winter of our childhood, was clear and sparkling and on many mornings fringed with a rim of ice, giving a promise of some natural exhilaration, though the stream only dwindled out to sodden potato fields under the limitless flat sky. Twice a day, at lunch and at six o'clock high tea, my mother took an earthenware jug and dipped water from the stream for the table. The water was delicious and cold enough to set the teeth on edge.

Once, I saw her stop in the deserted road and take a sip from the jug, as if that were a guilty thing to do.

In this household of strangers, my mother never quite knew what was her place or her role. My grandmother, though old, was still fit and hale, with a mind as sharp as her tongue, and from long practice she had a firm grip on all the simple routines of that house. Her children were all grown up and gone, and her husband knew better than to stray by much from the tracks laid out for him day by day. My grandmother's cold stare and resonant sniff were likely to stop him short in his wanderings. There were not many things needing to be done to keep that house ship-shape, and my grandmother did them according to her own settled ways.

My mother wanted to help but could not find the right things to do. That grim stare with its wealth of unspoken recrimination made my mother so nervous that her usually quick fingers fluffed the most simple task, leaving her open not only to the icy look but also to the condescending sneer. Suffering under this unreflective cruelty that the righteous impose upon their victims, my mother grew afraid of her mother-in-law. She retreated into the world of her children, gladly busying herself with the patching and snipping and sewing and darning needed to keep our reach-me-down secondhand wardrobe from raggedness. Then she turned unwanted attentions towards our persons – the unnecessary tying of a shoelace or tucking of an errant shirt-tail, the attack with brush and comb on tousled hair, the handkerchief ever-ready for a snotty nose, the prolonged scrub in the zinc bath on the kitchen floor, the hushing in the bedroom for fear of disturbing the old folk as we kids jostled and squealed under the puffy quilt at lights out.

She kept bedtime going as long as possible, demanding more

affection than youngsters are usually willing to give. We felt the oppressive warmth of too many kisses. Then she descended with heavy heart to sit, as it were, in the corner, in the solemn evenings of a tick-tocking clock and the ominous drip of the war news from the small bakelite radio on the dresser. Sometimes Churchill himself spoke to them in that slow, truculent growl that reduced the evil Hitler to the status of a mad clown. But most often catastrophe and disaster – it was the winter of 1940–41 – were mediated through the choked vowels of the BBC announcer.

Sometimes, my mother told me later, she was surprised to find herself quietly weeping.

She felt herself driven to look for housework, which was an irony for a girl with her history. In her youth she thought she had had enough of that for a lifetime. The whole tortuous trail of her early life had been an upward trajectory aimed to take her out of the mire of domestic labour – washing, scrubbing, polishing, ironing, dusting, cleaning, always cleaning. In India, when she had arrived there as nanny to the children of an Inspector of Indian Railways, she knew instinctively that she had at last kicked free from a certain submerged past. The gawky young officer, handsome enough but hopelessly maladroit, who had stepped on her toes at a Madras ball and thereafter pursued her with the hangdog perseverance of the poor scholarship boy on the rise, at least gave her a promise, seen in the shiny subaltern's pips on his shoulder and the masterly cut of his blue and scarlet mess-dress, of a final escape from the kingdom of grime, from chapped red hands and sore knees.

'How different this world is,' she thought, hearing of games and pranks, of how, during a parade, the pet monkey of the young officers shat on the wondrous hat of the colonel's wife. Oh how she laughed. Another future beckoned, graced by ease and leisure, peopled by a retinue of servants. The tinkling of the ice in the *chota peg* – the early-evening whisky and soda – heralded a more spacious gentility than the rough and tumble against lewd hands that she had previously endured in the shilling seats of some local cinema.

So, although she fled from my father, it was not so briskly that she could not be caught.

But now, in Lincolnshire, in this blighted wartime, she had been thrust back into a poor servitude, a crippled life, that bore comparison with her own beginnings. At the age of sixteen, after too many small family tragedies, she had been forced to abandon the luckless rural economy of the West of Ireland and make her way to England. There was nothing unusual in this, a course repeated time and again in families struck by misfortune or unemployment. Her father was dead; her eldest brother had gone down to tuberculosis; she was the eldest remaining child and there were five smaller ones for her mother to feed. There was a great need for money and it was accepted by all that she had a duty to take her poor qualifications to the labour-market in Ireland's hard-hearted but rich neighbour, sending home as much as she could afford out of her wages.

At first, she became a skivvy. There was nothing else available for someone as ill-prepared as a sixteen-year-old convent-educated country girl. The only prizes she had ever won at school had been for embroidery and needlework.

In bitter English lodgings she tried to keep alive some sense of the dignity of the past. She kept in her mind the image of the wide Mall in Castlebar, with the ample proportions of the Georgian façades, and her convent school at the end, in a mansion of some small-town grandeur formerly owned by the family of Lord Lucan. She recalled, in Westport, the little shop of her relatives, so snug and neighbourly by the running stream. She thought of her lazy young summers, scrambling the sunny scree above Clew Bay. She remembered her young brother, a boy-soprano standing out from Father Egan's choir at sung Mass to sing *Panis Angelicus*. She felt again in her bones the hard ascent of Croagh Patrick amid blustery showers, a crowd straining against the stones, united not only in religion but also by something beyond religion that connected their loneliness with the Inis Fail – the Island of Stones – of her homeland and with the coming of the Tuatha De Danann and the making of the hero-land. My mother was sentimental rather than religious, pious towards fables, though religion also entered into those fables. She knew her forebears on both sides of the family, tenant farmers with too few acres and small-time shopkeepers. She could count their lines for several generations. 'We are descended,' she later told me often enough when she was slightly tipsy, 'from the High Kings of Connacht.'

The nuns, and wretchedness, had whacked into her a notion of Holy Ireland.

But in her heart she knew that it was all a sham. Real Ireland left other feelings, more like wounds. She recalled the times of grief, one by one, when her mother brought forth a still-born baby or a little babe so tremulous in life that it expired within a few days. Wrapped in a lace shawl the tiny body let go and fell into a silence from which it had hardly emerged. Five times that had happened out of a total of twelve births. She remembered the gaunt cow out at her uncle's smallholding on the road to Bohola from whose TB-ridden milk her brother had caught the disease and died. She recalled the dangerous conviviality of her father, a farmer turned tailor who liked a drop and a flutter on the horses. Many times she had led him home with his arm about her shoulders and a soft look in his eye. She remembered another relative, an uncle dragged by the heels behind a Black and Tan cart, his head bouncing on the bumps of the roadway.

Most of all she remembered her father dead. He had been to Galway races on horseback. Returning in a state of jovial confusion, he had fallen from his horse somewhere between the Twelve Pins and Lough Corrib. The horse had bolted leaving her father with broken ribs and a punctured lung. He lay by the path for some time, into the evening chill, before a traveller found him. He lingered for a while but died from shock and pneumonia. He was not yet forty.

The death of the father left a hole in the family that had to be filled, by his widow's prayers of course, by any luck that might come their way, but most of all by grinding labour. My mother, as the eldest remaining child, became responsible for the young ones, washing, dressing, feeding, guiding, a counsellor for their doubts, a balm for their hurts, too tender for slaps but making their tears into her pain. Inside of two years she was worn to a scarecrow. She no longer skipped or sang or played tag or dares at the end of the Mall in the noisy ring of schoolgirls. By nightfall, she was too tired for the dancing that she loved best of all. She began to smoke, for the sake of her nerves. But still the household bills outran the family income. She took the packet-boat from Dun Laoghaire to Liverpool.

Talking of Ireland, she always used to say, 'It's a terrible place. It kills its own people. Anyway, the people are just a race of pygmies. What do they know of living?' After she left her homeland she returned only twice in a very long life, and then only for the shortest of visits.

In one respect my mother's early life gave her an advantage. She doted on children and had plenty of experience in looking after them. Within a short time in England she had progressed from skivvy to mother's help and then to nanny. She put herself in the hands of a London agency that specialized in providing, for a low wage, clean decent country girls with a religious education for the successful families of the Home Counties. She wore cotton print dresses with white cuffs and collars and a long grey coat nipped in at the waist to show her neat figure and slim build. She would stop before a shop window to pull a blue beret aslant above her light grey eyes and then go on with a certain swagger. She began to think better of herself.

She found that her services were in demand. In prosperous houses she lived in, partly superior servant and partly almost a member of the family. She had a room next to the children and a place at the table, though not for dinner parties. On these days she ate in the nursery or in the kitchen. For a happy period she worked for a novelist distantly related to the famous actress Sybil Thorndike, a thriller writer living in a house on the marshes amid a bohemian chaos of books. She began to read herself, something romantic but not too flighty, with a hint of tears in the inevitable pathos of true love.

Almost unconsciously she began to ape middle-class ways, digesting imperial prejudices and a new conservatism with the traditional Sunday dinners of roast beef and Yorkshire pudding. She took afternoon tea out of thin china cups, adding the milk before the straw-coloured Earl Grey. She read the *Express* or the *Mail*, not that *Mirror* rag, and found herself agreeing with the opinions of Lord Beaverbrook. She wore silk stockings. In the street, she no longer looked aside when a policeman's eye fell on her. She gave him a haughty look back. She learnt from her employers to be suspicious of Jews and had a horror of black people, of whom at this time she knew nothing. Her Irish accent slipped away as the language of middle England took its place, so slipshod and arrogant, full of sloppy diction and imprecisions drawled around a cigarette or over the rim of a cocktail glass. But all her life she still could not rid herself of the Irishness of certain words or phrases, like 'post office' or 'third-class'. Whereas she had once been voluble and quick in speech, now she let incomplete sentences drift. 'O you know what I mean,' she would say, and 'Well, there you are,' just like the English.

She went abroad, travelling with families on holiday or business. In Barcelona she was engaged by a millionaire Catalan banker as one of four 'governesses', of different nationalities, to look after his six children in a vast, stately apartment on the Paseo de Gracia. There was also a summer house hanging above the city heat, on the mountain top at Tibidabo. In the apartment, a Danish governess had stalked her through the gloomy maze of rooms. Beneath an oil-painting of senator or general brown with age my mother was cornered. A meaty Danish hand clenched her buttock and then full lips tried to kiss her on the mouth. My mother recoiled in shame and horror, for she knew nothing of lesbians and indeed didn't even know the word. The nuns had taught her that sex was a nasty business, unfortunately necessary for procreation, strictly in wedlock, to be endured but never to be indulged even in marriage. All her life, the thought of it left her disgusted and confused.

But so much work with children made her long for some of her own. She did not want a husband very much. Young men were for parties and demure flirting and picnics and dancing the night away. For ten years she had worked her own destiny and she had become too independent to welcome the rule of men with all their obsessive, wilful and infantile tricks. She abominated sexual fumblings, and the desperate panting pursuits aimed towards the bedroom. But she wanted children of her own, and according to the constitution of the society she had so carefully infiltrated there was no other way but wedlock. One just gritted the teeth and went ahead.

She prepared herself for it. India was lucky ground for her. In a sense, it provided her with a *tabula rasa* upon which she could rewrite her story. In India, all the English were strangers, imperial servants, starting on level terms more or less, without too much baggage from the past. Drawn together, a minority faced with nameless threats from a culture they did not understand and a history they misrepresented to themselves, the English felt the need for comradely bonds. The rigid stays of old hierarchies were loosened somewhat. It was possible for young people to become what they dreamed themselves to be. A son of a poor gardener became an army officer – a gentleman – and an Irish skivvy transformed herself into the officer's lady. To all their world, they became *sahib* and *memsahib*.

They married and entered fully into the life of the times. A handsome couple, and perhaps a happy one – he tall and quite dashing, she fey, impulsive, fun-loving. Two baby boys came in quick succession. An ayah was on hand for the drudgery of infancy, the bottles and the stinking nappies and the lacerated nights.

'We had nothing of course,' she used to say, 'but, oh what fun and gaiety!'

Mah-jong in the mornings, or the young wives' coffee parties; a gentle stroll out of the heat of the day on the maidan with the dog Kipper; charades and fancy dress; amateur dramatics; Sunday lunches at the club – *pulao* and long drinks – lasting well into the evening; the lovely mess-nights with the regiment, candles in silver sconces guttering under the slow swing of the *punkah*, the gleam of medals on broad chests, the rich tawny red of the circulating port, the fervent affirmation of the Loyal Toast; then the forgivable larks of the young officers, so puppy-like and endearing, barging about in childish games on the carpet.

At other times the crowd of them would get together at Luigi's Restaurant in Pindi before continuing with heated faces to the fashionable dance. Then they would ride out at dawn for a spin round the hill-top in an open cabriolet while some drunken voice attempted a melody from Bing Crosby, or that new soft-shoe transatlantic swing.

Her life went flying by, but my mother had not reckoned with Hitler and a world war.

*

What had happened to her hard-won advantages? She heard the night bombers drone out from the airfields of the fenlands nearby. Sometimes the noises of the air were so loud and puzzling she held her head in her hands. Those hands were again rough and sore, smelling of potato-peelings and cabbage-water. Testing the breakfast porridge with a finger she saw that her nail was broken and untrimmed. She could not laugh any more. Her children seemed always under her feet, and she did not know whether to hug them or smack them. Sometimes she did both in a minute. Her gums were beginning to bleed. She retired to bed in the afternoons with migraine headaches. Was she lacking in vitamins? Whom could she ask? Going in and out with a pail of pig-swill, she saw her mother-in-law silent behind the door or bent stiffly over the washtub, as impassive as a cigar-store Indian.

'Your grandmother was an upright and honest woman,' she told me with bitterness, 'but I could have hit her for her uncaring coldness to you and your brother and for her cruelty to me. Of course I didn't hit her, I was much too afraid of her.'

*

My mother could not endure so much hard-heartedness. The cold little cottage under the iron discipline of the old woman was like an angina in her chest. To free her breathing once again she took her brood under her wing and put us all for the time being in the upstairs rooms of the Rose and Crown pub.

In the mornings my brother and I went to the village nursery school. A handful of tiny tots with flat country accents tried to push wooden alphabet blocks into the simplest elements of an agricultural vocabulary – 'cow', 'pig', 'barn', 'hay'. Country schooling proceeds under different concepts, as well as a different sky, from that of the city. The retired lady who struggled as our teacher – too old for war-work – sang us rhymes in a cracked voice, keeping time with a pencil tapping a glass tumbler. The mid-morning mug of milk came warm from the day's first milking. In the afternoons, wrapped to the nose against the wind from the east, we learnt from the village kids the timeless arts of childhood mischief, how to defeat boredom with mud-slides and squabbles and trouble-making in farmyards. In the evenings, changed into pyjamas, we crouched on the landing of the pub, peering through banisters into the bar below.

The aroma that wafted up to us was peculiar. Damp coals, wet clothes, manure sticking to boots, a mustiness rubbed off from the coats of animals, the sourness of old farmhands who had long forgotten to bathe, all this mixed with the slop of the beer on the mahogany and the dry frowsty stink of the tobacco. But it was companionable in there, in the warm fug, with the light strained out and mellowed by the nicotine colour of walls and ceiling, with the rasp of hobnails on the scrubbed planks of the floor and the subdued, almost monosyllabic mumble of country talk, to outsiders hardly distinguishable from the soft grunts of their farm animals.

My mother liked to sit on a high stool at the end of the bar closest to the fire. The grate was small and the ration of coal not generous. She crossed her legs with some elegance and sat quietly, though the farmhands knew that she was Fred's wife and they could address her if they wished. They were in no hurry. She lit a cigarette and waited, expelling smoke quickly through her nose, taking a medium-dry sherry or a small whisky with a lot of soda.

We grew drowsy with the soft sounds and the clink of the glasses and went to bed. But we tried to keep awake until the bell rang for 'last orders'. Then we crept out again to the landing, getting ready to join our treble shouts to the landlord's traditional bellow of 'Time gentlemen, please'. This seemed worth all our efforts to keep awake. The adults, or so we thought, needed all the help they could get to steady them at the end of the day.

Once or twice while we were there, our grandfather sidled shyly into the public bar, having slipped the leash at home. Once, grandmother came to fetch him back. At the door of the bar – my grandmother would not enter – there was a muttered altercation.

'Tom,' she said with icy contempt, 'I can smell the drink on you.'

'Yus, missus, you can smell it right enough,' his battered old face beamed at her, 'but you cain't smell how many I've had!'

When my mother heard this exchange, she later said, she turned her head aside and laughed for the first time in weeks.

*

The jolly interlude did not last. Soon we were out in the flatlands, looking for somewhere more settled than a couple of rooms in a public house. It was unpleasant to discover just how dark was the world outside, away from the rough comfort and fellowship of the pub. Why was it that our life in the byways could not go on, pushing alphabet bricks into country words, singing 'Jack and Jill' with tremulous notes under a spinster's furrowed brow, sneaking tuppenny bars of bitter chocolate from the dusty counter of the village shop, lying down to sleep to the squeak of the beer-pulls and the soft thud of darts into the dart-board?

A ramshackle car took us to a bleaker reality. Out in dreary landscape we were dumped onto the rutted yard of Copse Farm where Farmer Griffith and his wife were prepared to rent us rooms but drew the line at extending to us anything like a welcome. Only the compulsion of the war drove them to rent out lodgings, but that cataclysm was not large enough to force them into friendliness.

I began to learn how much of farming was squalor. The long midden-heap behind the barn; the urine stench from the straw in the milking parlour; the thick coat of the farmyard dog matted with burrs and dried mud; rusted old machinery strangled by the weeds; green scum on the cattle-trough; fallen and split branches rotting in the orchard; broken gates stitched together with wire and baling-string; holes in the buckled tin roof of the tractor shed; the neglected farmhouse itself, blistered and blotched with weather marks. The ploughed fields shone dully, the colour of raw meat.

Mrs Griffith cooked turnips and swedes and beets in watery stews, with occasional hints of chicken or rabbit. A greyish bread was wrapped in plain paper. Meals were eaten in a general silence, with now and again a sharp word or two about the weather. It did not seem to be polite to mention the war. My brother and I scraped the plates, making as much noise as possible. We kicked each other under the table. After each meal Mr Griffith removed his false teeth and put them in a glass of water on the mantelpiece, and there they stayed in public view until the next meal. I had never seen detachable teeth before and went out of my way to give them a good inspection. They looked cruel and filthy, but I respected the farmer for his confidence in displaying them.

The farmhouse was cold, standing square in the way of the prevalent north-easterlies that swept down from Siberia. It was scarcely warmed by single-bar electric fires that could never be left on in a vacant room. The light bulbs were almost too dim for reading. Only a few fingers of hot water were allowed in the bottom of the bath. My brother and I grew morose, pushing and shoving to be first out of the house, lashing out at each other in sudden tempers. The vitality was draining out of us. Heads down, we kicked stones in the yard and poked sticks into the rabbit hutches. The animals learnt to avoid us. The dog warned us off with low growls, the muck-flecked hens flew apart clucking, and the geese, hissing with outstretched necks, got into a phalanx to repel us. The animals seemed as wretched as the farm.

One afternoon of bright winter sunshine Mr Griffith slaughtered a pig. It was a big sow with floppy ears and what looked to me even then a worried expression. I was surprised by the two remarkable rows of its teats. The farmer and a labourer despatched it with brutal efficiency, not caring whether we children were watching or not. Executions of the farmyard were no mystery to the country child – chickens with necks wrung, rabbits stunned and killed, partridges shot for the pot. The pig, squealing and backing and sliding in the mud, often down on its knees, was jammed in a metal frame and its throat expertly cut with one long motion of the knife. A bloody bubble like a sigh burst from its mouth. Then the hind feet were secured by a rope to a block and tackle and the up-ended beast was hitched up to a beam over the barn door, and left there for the blood to drain. After the first rush, a thin frothy flow leaked into the bucket beneath.

At the end of the winter at Copse Farm I fell ill. Despite a warning from my brother I had been larking about on the rim of the cattle-trough and I had fallen into three feet of dirty, icy water. Though fished out quickly, and bathed, and sent to bed with red flannel and a hot-water bottle on my chest, I went down with pneumonia, which my mother attributed to congenital bronchial weakness. In my fever I saw nightmares, a naked rabbit wearing its own flayed skin like an ill-fitting overcoat, and a recurring vision of a pig thrashing and drowning in a pool of blood.

The doctor said, under the circumstances, bad dreams were not unexpected. I had a high fever, and besides it was wartime. Horrors were normal enough. With many patients to see, the doctor left in a hurry. I heard the farmyard gate groan on rusty hinges and clang behind him.

THREE

Corridors

Another departure, another cold destination. Money was the problem. While we were in Lincolnshire, two or three times my mother had found it necessary to go to London to see the bank manager.

A railway journey, in those days, with the trains flushed from their normal routes by bomb damage and troop movements, was like a prolix argument set down in broken grammar. Trains puzzled by their own tracery grumbled over a destabilized railbed, metal squealing even on the slowest of curves. In the carriages, smuts from the engine lay on the dirty rep of the seats. Weather streaks obscured the windows and a greyish grit coated most surfaces. Water in the lavatory, if it ran at all, came from the tap in brown driblets.

In an old photo I see my mother arriving under the hooting, echoing, dingy canopy of the London terminus, a pert little town-hat at a cockeyed angle on her head and a tentative smile on her pale face. The day had hardly begun and already she looked wan and pasty.

On all sides in London were mementoes of old wars. War is the one big game common to all complex societies at all times. The evolution of modern man is set out in the streets of our cities as a true *via dolorosa*, by way of fire and sword and bullet. How much public commemoration stinks of death! Implacable generals with a full book of killings sit proudly on frantic horses, all arched neck and flaring nostrils and bulging eyes. Swords are uplifted, pikes aimed at bellies, gun-barrels levelled with terrified faces. Cannons thrust their heavy snouts skywards. Women carved in stone, with wild weeping hair, disrobe out of pity for the fallen.

At the bottom of Lower Regent Street, Florence Nightingale with her lamp, under the grim visages of three hairy guardsmen, pointed my mother towards the door of Cox & King's, a bank once brought to its knees by the accumulated debts of all those sad young officers smashed in the trenches of the Great War. Now this old institution was subsumed under the bulk of a large national bank but still, as it were, acting as its military branch. Here Mr Reynolds, a lively gnome with a bony bald head and heavy glasses, awaited her.

My mother was not good with money. Prodigal with her left hand, she grew guilty at expense and became tight-fisted with her right hand. Costs crept up on her and took her by surprise. She had been used to the cheap prices of India, and an airy way of living. In wartime England she could never quite determine what was a necessity and what was an indulgence – a bowl of soup in Lyons Corner House, a winter vest, shoes for growing boys, lipstick in a new colour, a Penguin paperback of Priestley or Compton Mackenzie. A packet of Benson & Hedges rather than the cheaper Woodbines? Her husband started the war as a captain in an Indian regiment where the rates of pay were not calculated to support a family life in England. He remitted what he could but payments were sometimes delayed and always not enough. Adrift with two young children in the wash of war, in a land that was not hers and where she could make very few claims, my mother found herself in the midst of preoccupied people, harried by dangers, fears and worries, kind enough in intention but without the time or energy to take on the woes of others. After a struggle against her finances she collapsed into debt and appeared before Mr Reynolds in trepidation, feeling like a child caught with fingers in the sweetie-jar.

Mr Reynolds was an old-fashioned bank manager, formal in dress and speech, punctilious as to detail, calm and authoritative in decision. He was also, in my mother's eyes, something of a saint. He took a lofty view. What was a small amount of debt, in the cir-cumstances? There was security, in the form of my father's regular salary, which was likely to grow with promotions, if he could avoid getting killed. A modest sum now would be enough to tide her over, even though she had the expensive responsibility of small children – food, clothes, lodgings, education, as well as little easements to compensate for sad times. Trust Mr Reynolds, he knew. In the meantime, he said, she might look for a little job, for extra income and for peace of mind. 'Secure the home front, so to speak,' he told her, glasses twinkling. 'There are plenty of wartime tasks waiting to be done by smart young ladies.'

So we packed and went on. We turned our backs on the long slough of mud and misery that Lincolnshire had become for us and came to a new place of rest, standing on the up-platform of Oxford station, two scuffed leather suitcases in hand, and with a future as cloudy as March skies.

*

Then lengthening days and the change of season brought in stiff breezes and skies crinkly with driven cloud and a weak sunlight licking at the damp patches on the pavement. We wanted to take it as a promise of better days.

On a certain morning we found ourselves standing before a high iron gate. Once again I had a firm grip on my mother's hand, edging around behind her skirts to place a barrier between me and whatever this fate might be. My bolder brother had put on the responsible front of seniority, though I could see he was frowning with his underlip nipped between his teeth. The gate before us was heavy and black, embellished with blobs of metal which, beneath the thick coats of paint, might represent fruit or bombs – pineapples or grenades. On each side an interminable wall strode out of sight, rising powerfully above the narrow pavement. We boys were in some kind of uniform, shorts and jackets in a serge cloth, long woollen socks, ties fumbled around our necks. The coarse material of the clothes made us itch. We were self-conscious, wondering what new trial or game all this stiffness and formality heralded.

Our mother tugged on a bell-pull and we heard a muffled clang within. A long pause and then the gate swung slowly inward. A lady in a coif and a black robe and a severe starched wimple stood before us. I could not bring myself to look into her face, which was withdrawn and shaded by the strange headgear. So I concentrated about the level of her waist where a large bunch of keys dangled from a thin leather belt. She reached forward to shake my mother's hand, offering her own hand that was big and callused, with swollen

knuckles. A boxer's hand. She turned and with very few words led
us into a dark panelled hall shot through with a single shaft of
brightness from a statue of a gaudy lady in pink and blue plaster. It
was a shock to me to see that this lady had her heart exposed in her
breast with golden rays emanating from this terrible wound. Only a
day or two later, with my ear twisted for my ignorance, did I learn
that this sorry apparition was the Blessed Virgin, a lady in some way
connected (though I had as yet no idea of the details) with God.
Doubtful to begin with, I started to sink under the painful puzzle of
it all. The human figures, like the statue, were remote from my
experience, the meaning was beyond me. Low mumbles passed
between my mother and the nun, who finally essayed a brief, taut
smile.

Then we were turned over to those boxer's hands.

*

In this time of war various arms of the government, seeking some
safety outside London, had colonized many of the towns within easy
reach of the capital. An administrative branch of the Foreign Office
had come to rest in Oxford, and here my mother found a position
as a temporary filing clerk. The job was not demanding. A few
ladies, mostly young wives bound by national solidarity and a
genteel education, distributed pieces of paper and made cups of tea.
My mother had the qualifications, which hardly went beyond the
ability to read and write, and earned approval as an officer's wife (the
Foreign Office was notoriously snobbish). The job suited her well
enough – some chatter and giddiness among the solemn civil
servants of the FO persuaded a young woman inexperienced in
official ways that she was part of national destiny. Her tasks filled the
tedious hours of her arrested life, gave her a little extra income, and
distracted her from the sense of her own unhappiness. But to take up
this position she had had to get her children off her hands, and that
had meant placing them in a boarding school, preferably a Catholic
one.

My mother was Catholic by instinct, tradition and upbringing,
but she did not care for doctrine or theology and devised her own
rules of daily practice. She thought that a public acknowledgement
of her Catholicism and a strong suspicion of all other sects and faiths

would be enough for heaven. Here on earth she would do much as she pleased, relying on the simple morality of a peasant heart. Years later, she told me that the only time she had been to church during the long years of her marriage had been for the wedding Mass itself. Yet she had insisted, as a condition of marriage, that my father take instruction and be received into the Catholic Church. Seeing that her religion was a matter of culture and prejudice, not under-standing, my father had simply given way. With some amusement and more impatience he had gone through the childish rote of the catechism while sharing a few whiskys with a benevolent Irish priest, sitting on the verandah of the parish house as the Indian sunset burned into the distant plain. Then he forgot the whole business. He remained what he had always been, the sturdy agnostic who at a young age had chosen to pump the organ-bellows of the Methodist chapel from outside rather than listen to the preaching from within.

The nuns of her convent in Ireland had been for my mother nightmare shadows in the dark dream of her childhood. Despite this, she knew with certainty that an order of nuns was the only institution fit to undertake the education of little children who were, at least nominally, Catholic. Besides, where else could she find a boarding school willing to take kids as young as four or five?

The Convent of the Sacred Heart, by the river on the outskirts of Oxford, for a suitable fee received little boys into the rigorous circle of its conviction, and released my mother into the world of wartime work.

*

From the first, the sense of space appalled me. The ceilings were too high, the doors too tall, the rooms too big. They petered out in extremities where the gloom bunched in corners as impenetrable as jungles. Ill-lit corridors, hardly touched by daylight, ran out of sight like slow murky rivers. Sounds were dampened, a world with a finger on its lips, reduced to sighs and mutters. Overwhelmed by this scale I was afraid to look up but stumbled on with eyes on the floor, driven into place by gruff orders, digs of the elbow, or a tug on the sleeve.

From morning to night the nuns began to discipline our days. Growth requires some routine, but this weary stamp of regularity marked me beyond my tender years and I wept for my small lost freedoms. I relinquished the dozy hours of former days, when I had fed ducks in the park, kicked a tin can down an alleyway, mooched the street with a stick ringing against iron railings, or in idle moments before bed had leafed through a picture book in front of the glowing embers of the fire. For this abandoned life, I snivelled under the bedclothes after lights-out in the convent dormitory, or in the raw damp jakes, contemplating my chapped knees in the fraction of the day set aside for a satisfactory bowel movement.

The young child cries for the comfort of a mother, but we wept into the void. There was a remote and fearful figure known as the Mother Superior, but none of our tears stained the black-clad expanse of her forbidding breast.

A clap of hands at an early hour brought us awake in the dimness of the dormitory. Speechless, we dressed, then formed a silent line of midgets in ill-fitting clothes (in those days of rationing, to make clothes last longer, our suits were bought a size too big). At a sharp order we shuffled off, hair still unkempt, kicking the heels of those in front.

'Eenie, meenie, Mussolini,' we hissed behind the nun's back, 'hurry up you silly ninny.'

'Silence, children,' snapped Sister Mary Bede. 'We do not make a noise as we approach the House of God.'

A ragged line of shrunken figures we clumped downstairs in heavy shoes so insecurely tied that half the laces dragged. Our footfalls on the worn parquet floors made a dull, lowering clatter, leaden with hesitation and regret.

'Move along now, children. We haven't got all day. You, slow-coach, get up here with you, or it'll be the worst for you.'

And Sister Mary Bede, taking a powerful pincer grip on the ear of some poor laggard, would drag him forward wailing into the refectory.

Watery tea poured from large tin pots. Only one teaspoon of sugar per cup was permitted. Sister's eagle eye was on us.

'Stir your tea clockwise,' she warned. 'The other way is the devil's way.'

The rules of the table were exacting. Backs straight, no slumping on the benches. No elbows on the table. Chew each mouthful twenty times, mouth closed, hands folded quietly on the lap. A thin spread of marmite on the bread was allowed at breakfast, a scrape of jam at tea. The jam, roughly of a strawberry type, was rumoured to be made of marrow, artificially flavoured, with little pits added for effect. On Sundays, there was a sticky but pleasant stuff called peanut butter. Porridge with horrid lumps was a detested staple. Nothing could be refused, and all food had to be eaten.

'Remember the starving children of Europe,' Sister admonished. 'What wouldn't they give for such delicious food? Don't let me see as much as a crumb left on your plate.'

War could not afford the luxury of waste, and to express a preference in these times was a selfish act bordering on the sinful. When one of the parents brought in an iced birthday cake, to be shared among the children as an exceptional treat, Sister descended on those who left the icing and the marzipan to the last and swept the longed-for delicacies from their plates. 'God,' she sniffed, 'does not send His gifts for you to pick and choose.'

Every act was measured against the iron rod of religion. At the centre of our lives stood the mystery of faith. In the convent, the chapel dominated the buildings and regulated all the activities of the day. Everything we did circled round it or pointed to it. For me, it became a place of dread. When the great oak door opened, with a stealthy quiet that belied its bulk, the unwholesome perfume of stale incense pinched my nostrils. The wink of the sanctuary lamp – a wizard's eye – made the heart skip with apprehension. In the cave of the church sombre light drifted onto heavy fittings, lying like dark dross between the pews. Pushed into those pews in rows we clutched at one another for support, forgetting our usual bickering and glad for once of human contact. From the hard bench I watched the strange man in the vestments mouth at the altar the magic Latin words that we did not understand. His gestures were languid and mournful, while the servers in lace-fringed white surplices soft-footed around him in a slow but difficult dance.

In the small morning hours, or in the tired dusk of evening, it was hard to take it all in. Solemnity is a drug of a kind, a hypnotic. Even so, our attention often wandered. A tired child would fall into a doze, head lolling on a neighbour's shoulder. Others gaped into the great spaces of the roof, or stared at plaster saints with haloes of tarnished gilt. Candles in clusters, gummed with molten wax, waited to be lit by the matches of suppliants.

Then, with the climax of the Mass approaching, the nuns drove us to our knees with fierce whispered reminders or with a knuckle poked in the back of the neck. The priest raised the Host in the air to the tinkle of a tiny bell. I did not know what this gesture meant. It looked like some petition or pleading. But I recognized in the weight of the uplifted arms a sadness beyond tears but also beyond my understanding.

The big oak door opened again and let us out, from interior dark to the grey light of ordinary day. Going back and forth between these two worlds I learnt that there were two Gods (the third one of the Trinity was a conundrum beyond even our powers of belief). The first, the grim emaciate on the Cross above the altar, all wounds and bones, was the Inflexible Judge, the Prince of Rigour, the Frightener of Souls, served by hard-minded monitors with rods in the hand. The second, the one whom Sister Catherine called Gentle Jesus, was the obverse of the divine coin, the Redeeming Comforter, the Balm for the Hurt. It was for the sake of this Gentle Jesus that Sister Catherine urged us to give our few pennies of pocket money towards the upkeep of the African missions.

'Who'll give thruppence to save a black piccaninny?' said Sister Catherine to our class with cheerful red-faced enthusiasm, waving a kindly arm across the broad expanse of the African map.

I loved to see how Sister Catherine's ample flesh jounced when she was jolly and excited so I gave all my thruppenny bits for Africa. I was convinced (since money had no relevance in our lives beyond paying for a sweet or a glass marble) that I had *purchased* a number of black babies – a little family flock that was mine – and this thought gave me warm feelings of friendly possession and belonging that I longed for but lacked in the convent. Gentle Jesus had sent me my own imaginary companionship – a squall of tiny jungle tots – to compensate for the cold harsh discipline imposed under the agonized stare of the Judge on the Cross.

Our only hope for relief from this severity was to hide beneath the cloak of Gentle Jesus. But the way to forgiveness was not easy to find; it was hedged and blocked by the thorns of observation. The black monitors were ever-vigilant and He on the Cross was not deceived. The nuns were very free in their interpretation of His displeasure:

'God does not love naughty children.'

'Nose-picking in church is an insult to heaven.'

'Only a sinful boy scribbles on his picture book.'

'Neglect your prayers and you'll get no blessings.'

'Every act of disobedience is another wound in His side.'

'The fires of hell await little liars.'

'God punishes bed-wetters.'

And if admonition and threats had no effect, then came the clinching argument against which there was no appeal. 'What Sister says, child, is God's law.'

Though heaven demanded so much, the rules of conduct here on earth, even if certain, were obscure. Both punishments and rewards flowed from the Church, imposed, granted or withdrawn by inscrutable religious authority. My brother, leaving his pew to follow a small trail of fellow pupils to the altar rail for their First Communion, was stopped in horror, hauled away by the shoulder with much finger-wagging, and returned at once to the ranks of the sinners, because he had not yet made his First Confession. As a punishment, his advance to the altar rail was put off to some unspecified time. He remained among a graceless herd while smarter boys put an early foot on the road to heaven. In another case, when in a playground fight I split my brother's forehead with a brick, I was removed from the group of boys learning to be Mass-servers. I was denied the holy foppery of lace and candlelight, incense and bells. In this way I was prevented from giving my fullest service to the Lord. This was a dire punishment for any faithful son of the Church. It was true. I was not much of a servant for the Lord. I was sad and bemused and given to fits of violence. The nuns, with their threats of divine displeasure, somehow failed to cure my outbursts of temper. I wanted my mother.

★

'What would you like to do today?' said my mother in a hopeless voice we had come to know so well.

We never had an answer to this, but it did not matter to us that we were drifting without much purpose. The important thing was that we were away from the convent for the afternoon. If the day was fine we would wander. Nowhere in particular. Magdalen Bridge to Carfax. Peeping in the austere wartime shops of the High, past crouching pubs with low, battered doorways and windows of bottle-glass. Amusements for children at this time were in short supply. We took in the modest stock of sights – Radcliffe Camera, Sheldonian, Bodleian, Ashmolean – those pompous names for quite innocent institutions. Then we made our way towards open spaces, under a sky that seemed always more welcoming than the wan pall of grey or watery blue that hung over the convent playground. We skirted the Botanic Gardens into Christ Church Meadow, or aimed for the Parks in a green, almost drowned landscape, strange territory where rivers seemed to change their names at will and a place called Mesopotamia lay, as it were, offshore. But best of all for us were the gardens of Worcester College, which revealed, though I did not know it then, a view of the subtle artifice of the European imagination.

If it rained there was nothing for it but to eke out time in a café, reading and re-reading the timid offerings of the wartime menu, and settling almost inevitably on Heinz tinned spaghetti in tomato sauce, a dish known to us as 'worms on toast'. My mother wrinkled her nose in disgust. She hated vulgarity.

I look now at a photo of her from that time. Heavy coils of fair hair gathered at the back of the neck, pale widely spaced eyes, a long upper lip trembling on the edge of a smile. There is an air of diffidence but a hint also of some new woman emerging beneath.

In Oxford she began, as she said, 'to come out of herself'. With colleagues from her office she went to a concert or two, though she preferred operetta. 'Such fun,' she would say, 'such gaiety.' She was not musical though she would hum along strenuously to well-known classical pieces – Beethoven's Fifth or the Tchaikovsky fiddle concerto – getting the turns of the melody wrong and beating time on the arm of her chair. She did have a remarkable memory for the voices of famous singers and gained herself some artistic credit by recognizing at once Galli-Curci or Conchita Supervia or Lily Pons.

She would cock her head aside like an attentive bird. 'Ah, dear Richard Tauber,' she would murmur dreamily. Was it the voice or the fame of the singer that met her approval?

On the whole, the theatre pleased her more. She had an eye for fame here also, and later she used to speak of seeing 'that young Coral Browne' at the Playhouse. She attended most weeks for a diet of Pinero, Coward, Rattigan. She was suspicious of Shaw. Too Irish, too wordy, too argumentative, he invited cynicism and disbelief. 'So clever-clever,' she said disparagingly. Wilde was Irish too, and witty perhaps, but he laid souls bare in a most uncomfortable way. My mother liked to live in a nice world, with indecencies hidden. The motives of the propertied classes – those founts of authority – should not be exposed. 'Heartless,' she called Wilde – a grave criticism, for she attached great store to the heart. Shakespeare, apart from the whimsical comedies, she did not care for. The barbarism of murder, rape, treachery, madness, eye-gouging seemed to her grotesquely medieval. The power of ungovernable emotion was a distressing affliction. She wanted to turn her eyes from the spectacle, not investigate it. 'We've come a long way from those days,' she would say after the war, abandoning in some byway of memory Auschwitz and Stalingrad and the Dresden fire-storm and the nuclear night of Hiroshima, and even the bombs of the Blitz that fortunately did not fall on Oxford.

She never wanted to delve below the surface. Life down there was unbearably raw. 'Why can't people be pleasant?' she used to lament. 'It's so easy.' Her simple job at the Foreign Office gave some shape to her day, some stability. After that, she innocently craved what she called 'fun'. She wanted to hold her head up, floating, in a world of knights and maidens. But she looked down and saw her feet churning the muck and refuse of a brutal civilization.

Most of all, when the evening freed her from the office, she loved to dance. She was poised and stylish on the dance-floor, keen to try the latest steps, and she reaped many compliments. When the American officers began to arrive in Oxford towards the middle of the war, my mother met these energetic young men, with their curious courtesy and unquenchable enthusiasm, in the bar of the Randolph Hotel. Her children were in boarding school. What could be wrong in going to a dance now and again? These young Americans seemed so eager and desperate to please. Surely they were officers and gentlemen?

So whatever the calls of the next morning, when an occasion came she would dance most of the night away, head high, eyes lighted on some blissful region of grace and movement, her partner held affectionately but at a proper distance. And if some green young fellow, aching with loneliness and giving way to the seduction of the dance, tried to get fresh, my mother was disturbed and frightened. She would break away in alarm and rush to the ladies' room, her eyes brimming with tears. It was the world getting in the way again. Why couldn't people be *nice*?

The world, of course, was very far from nice. Just when she thought her life was in some equilibrium, she was thrown into turmoil once more. It was too difficult to make the equation of happiness balance. The bad moments struck out the good. The bleak lodging off the Woodstock Road where she sat on empty evenings, trying to overcome the static on her radio, clutching misery about her like a shroud. The grubby kitchenette for the lodgers at the end of the passage, rustling with angry draughts, where she opened tins of spam and powdered egg (in one can she discovered a dead mouse), and stared in dismay at slabs of whalemeat. The shuffling of ration-cards, trying to work out when she would have enough points for a new dress. Queueing for everything, feeling the wetness of the pavement creep into the cracked soles of her shoes. Where was the money to mend them, with so many other calls on her purse?

Waiting for the bus, and on the long slow drives to the convent, she would reflect on the unhappiness of her children and how painful that was for her.

'Oh how I suffered for you poor darlings,' she told me later, 'but I felt it was for the best. And besides, what else could I do?'

Her own helplessness absolved her from any responsibility for our grief.

The school holidays were the worst times for her. Whatever could she do with us? By chance, the husband of the manageress of the Randolph Hotel, a wartime soldier, was one of my father's junior

officers in the Middle East. For the school holiday a place was found
for us in the hotel, a grand double bedroom with a bathroom
attached, at a special low rate. We would eat in the restaurant. This
generous arrangement was a great relief for my mother but her
satisfaction did not last long. Released from the convent I could not
control my pent-up rage. It flowed from me like lava through the
quiet dim spaces of the hotel, boiling into the hush of the writing-
room and lounge, crashing like dropped pans and smashed crockery
amid the snowy covers of the restaurant, finally expending itself at
bedtime in an exhausted hysteria, the gasps of a disturbed child
clinging to the pillow for safety. After several days of this, my mother
smacked me on the bottom with the back of a hairbrush. Then she
fainted.

Soon we both knew that we could not continue to live at this high
pitch of drama. Nor could the hotel afford our presence. My brother
and I returned to the convent and arrangements were made for us to
stay there during future holidays.

'I wept when I had to leave you,' my mother confided later, 'but
you were such a handful. I couldn't do a thing with you, and you
made me so unhappy. What I did, I thought it was for the best.'

★

So we knew we were different. Other children went home for the
holidays. We were abandoned to realms of silence and dust. Shifting
aimlessly between empty rooms we hesitated in corridors, weighed
down under the shadows and gloom of those long tunnels that
seemed both a part and a cause of our despair. Often they led to
mystery or to forbidden territory, to locked doors, dead-ends or
notices saying PRIVATE and NO ENTRY. In these places we took to
talking in whispers, haunted by dreads that we could not resolve into
the clear light of day. Other children had homes. We had the
corridors, or certain specified rooms left unlocked and void, with
too many hard chairs arrayed around the walls and threadbare carpets
that spoke of penury and dearth. Outside, the playground mocked
us with memory of childish uproar. We threw stones, or squabbled
half-heartedly, or dug in the sandpit, too dejected to make anything
better than holes.

At night, still whispering, we told each other stories, trying to console ourselves with fantasy as we awaited the oblivion of sleep. We were the sole occupants of ghostly dormitories. The other beds were stripped bare, the place smelling of pine-scented disinfectant. The plaster statue of Christ at the end of the room was shrouded in a white sheet. In the night, I woke often, drifting in the vast darkness. Going to the lavatory I stumbled back bemused by the dead rows of beds. My heart thudded at the increasing muddle in my head. Where was my bed? I could not find my way and curled up like a foetus onto the nearest mattress. When we opened our eyes we saw morning light dribble through the big east window onto the shrouded Christ standing as the sentinel of the day.

Set apart in this way, we began to value our difference from others, even though we suffered for it. How had it come about? We were refugees clinging, in this sepulchral world, to a faint memory of heat and light in the India of our birth, though in my own case the memory of the past was so unformed that I had to take it on trust from my elder brother. From time to time this conviction was confirmed by a sudden surprise, such as the arrival of a box of Turkish Delight as a gift from our father in the desert. The spongy jelly, perfumed with attar of roses and covered with a light dust of sugar-powder, seemed to us like a promise deferred.

Such a promise was thin fare to live on. In the meantime I was realizing the worst fears of Sister Mary Bede. My temper was becoming uncontrollable. I was a little liar. I began to wet my bed. I was a naughty child and God did not love me.

FOUR

Banana Man

GRIPPED BY RELIGIOUS discipline, both in term-time and in holidays, I grew used to a daily life of small dangers – arbitrary and sneaky punishments, petty meannesses, little mind-controlling tyrannies. We all became wary, recognizing the signs of trouble: the stealthy swish of long black robes, the click of rosary beads; the harsh intake of breath and the command to stop *at once*, followed by an enraged middle-aged face thrust towards us, framed by the weird bonnet of the wimple; then the scolding, in a fierce undertone, often accompanied by a good shaking – '*stupid* child, *naughty* boy, *wicked* little nuisance' – which led to the rap of a ruler across the knuckles, or banishment to stand in a dark corner, or the long trek to an early bed without supper.

After a time I no longer knew that life could be otherwise. I was inured to misery, which became endurable so long as it avoided actual bodily pain. Life was bleak, but were not greyness and emptiness the colour and the shape of the times? 'Some little boys,' Sister Mary Bede used to say with heavy emphasis, 'will never learn when they're well off.' I acknowledged what seemed to be the facts, hard though they were.

So I accepted the judgement of the nuns on my own behaviour, being forced, in the usual manner of childhood, to navigate by the only moral map available, the one licensed by guardians and teachers. But I came to feel, in loneliness and the peculiarities of our situation, that I was marked out, set apart from the common lot. It was a distinction of a kind, and I learnt to take comfort from it. The daily blows and insults became easier to withstand. They were seen, most perversely, as marks of status. In the battles of the playground, in the everlasting boyhood contests between Cowboys and Indians, between Authority and Defiance, I knew instinctively which side I was destined to be on. For was I not, both by birth and present circumstance, a person separated out, a natural 'Indian'?

To be different becomes a source of secret pride.

★

I did not understand much about prayer, though we were only too often on our knees. But I knew well enough what it was to beg. We all learnt how to do that. Roused into the sombre shadows of another shoddy morning we begged for a few more moments of sleep. In timid voices we asked for an extra slice of bread and a spoonful of jam. Hopping from foot to foot we shot up our hands for leave to go to the lavatory. In the winter, denied permission to wear gloves and forbidden to put our hands in our pockets, we tucked frozen hands into our armpits. Indoors, we tried to thaw out by sitting on the hot radiators, though this too was not permitted for fear of getting piles. Often reduced to tears, we would hold out ashamed hands for a handkerchief. As we sniffled and wiped our eyes our creased and anxious little faces appealed for more kindness and fewer slaps. And of course we continually begged, either in the confessional or under a nun's basilisk gaze, for forgiveness of our many sins.

There was so much to ask for. In fact, all my obstructive, morose and violent behaviour was a petition begging for my release.

Then that release came suddenly, for reasons that were hidden to me. In summer towards the end of the war our family moved from Oxford to the south Dorset coast. This move indicated, I suppose, an easing of our money worries. My father, a professional soldier with plenty of pre-war experience, had risen rapidly in wartime, and his pay went up with his rank. For me, quitting the low-lying Thames river-valley that was so intimately connected with the fever-haunted, almost hallucinatory oppression of the convent was only another mysterious shift of fate.

Now even the weather seemed kinder – the bracing sea airs, the dash of spray off the breaking waves, the sun glinting like hide and seek between driven clouds. A new mood settled on my mother, one of almost dangerous complacence. Her walk had a swing to it, as if she were now on her way with some purpose. She shed her dowdy suit – the appropriate wear for the Foreign Office – and took to flowery summer frocks with sandals on her feet. Her hair, once closely pinned up, was now looser and often wind-blown. She smiled, lingered in company, and forgot to annoy us with her fidgeting and her nervous fears for our safety. In her own estimation she deserved a rest (could not the whole of England say that also?).

She took a room in a small hotel in Uplyme and prepared to bring her life back in line with her own sense of normality. For her, that meant being wife and mother. No matter that her husband was fighting a war two thousand miles away and her children were shut up in a boarding school. She regarded these circumstances as somehow unreal, having to do with a shadow-life of wartime, whereas her real life, modelled on her past days in India, lay in the return to India. No longer burdened with the drudgery of office work, for which she was almost wholly unsuited, she could now devote herself to the thought of the future. There was much domestic business to take in hand. Most of our family goods had gone to the bottom of the sea in 1940. Her little world of household effects had to be re-gathered, packed and stored.

Then it was necessary to recuperate her health and her looks and her good humour. She relaxed. No need to get up quite so early in the morning. No need to join the bus queue, to jostle with crowds for a hasty lunchtime sandwich, to tread pavements homewards to the stark suburban room, fumbling shillings for the one-bar electric fire, staring in hopeless resignation at the faded regency stripes of the wallpaper and the stain of the water-leak in the corner of the ceiling that looked like a map of Nowhere. And no need also to fret herself ill out of worry for her children.

We too, her children, were busy getting acquainted with a type of normality that was new to us. From the popish dark of the convent, so baroque and un-English and blighted by a suspect religious enthusiasm, we were put into the care of the English middle-class system of private schooling. Though we did not know it, we were exchanging the subtle intellectual cruelties of the Jesuitical Counter-Reformation for the hearty violence of Dr Arnold's Anglo-Saxon invention, a regime still bearing the imprint of the whiskered old goat himself, with his love of floggings and cold baths and many hours on the muddy playing fields.

This was a part of our English bourgeois inheritance. And it was not hard to see that there was a certain grandeur to it. An imposing gateway, with tall stone piers and a wrought-iron gate thrown open, embraced us with a large gesture. Then a long driveway marched boldly through the pitches of the games fields to a gravel circle before the front door of a big eccentric Victorian house. The house had been built with all the lapses of an over-rich, whimsical domestic taste, but was now transformed into a school with too many odd compromises for either convenience or comfort. From the front door, the main passage was lined with hunting trophies, the large heads of slaughtered animals, their old fur scruffy with dust and bald patches and the glass eyes looking unbearably despondent. Another place, an administrative office off the passage, had walls prickly with the tines of many antlers.

Unavoidable draughts swept through the house, enough to please even the most austere of muscular Christians. Great, rattling windows seemed to sail over the sea. The views were magnificent. From the dormitories, clattering with wind noise, we looked across rabbit-bitten turf and over the low cliff to the sun setting out in the dizzy vista of the ocean. We were tempted to hug ourselves, though unsure whether from cold or wonder.

In the convent, we had inhabited a world of sullen whispers, sidelong glances, secretive, cautious, withdrawn. Our new world was ringing with loud halloos, voices perpetually raised, doors slammed, feet stamped, instructions roared as if from passing ships. Our amusement in the convent had been solitary and painstaking and private. In our new school we were taught the steamy satisfaction of corporate effort, how to work for a team, and take our knocks like little men, without complaint. Strange English excesses, such as cricket, were revealed to us by sport-besotted schoolmasters. Footballs were kicked around, not in the wild chaotic rushes of the convent playground, but with the communal aim of goal-scoring in view.

The convent had taken the individual soul in hand, for rigorous discipline on the road to heaven. Our new masters looked askance at that. It sounded to them selfish and ungentlemanly. Teamwork was what mattered. Play the game and life would follow from it.

At last, I was beginning to get the hang of how to be English.

In a short time, adaptable as most schoolboys, we had learnt to fit in. Only our Catholicism held us apart. There were no other Catholics in the school, but our peculiarity was treated with the respect that a liberal tradition gives to puzzling metaphysical anomalies. On Sundays, my brother and I put aside the hard-boiled eggs from our breakfast – the ration was one fresh egg each per week – and we set out alone for Mass in a nearby village.

In good weather we went across the fields, stopping to crack our egg-shells on the stone pillar of the gatepost. On weekends, nothing disturbed the tranquillity of the wartime countryside. No traffic, the farm tractors at rest. Working men with their boots unlaced pottered amid the vegetable patch, a full pot of tea on the hob. A woman sat in the sun with her skirt hitched up on her thighs, shelling peas into a white colander. Thin cigarette smoke rose over a hedge.

Penned up in the convent, or slouching about the Oxford streets, I had formed no conception of nature, apart from the artful formalities of Worcester College gardens. I began to clear my eyes and cleanse my ears for the benefit of the natural world around me – the trill and the squeak and the caw of the birds, soft animal grunts in the undergrowth, scurrying of small beasts, kamikaze buzzing, iridescent flashes of tiny wings, the changing green palette of the woodland – all this was a surprise.

We were, as our schoolmasters gravely told us, in a state of 'total war'. If we found a pen or a cigarette lighter or some little packet on the beach, we were drilled never to pick it up. It might be a booby trap. I could not reconcile these versions of the world. How was it possible to connect the dreamlike but enduring reality of Sundays with the brutal temporal fears of weekdays?

We had no lessons to teach us the meaning of angst, or existential doubt. Instead, we had cold showers and a brisk trot around the playing field.

★

In the holiday, a small girl about my own age was staying, like us, at the hotel in Uplyme. She was wiry and lively, with two fair plaits hanging to her shoulders. She giggled a lot, staring into my face quizzically before skittering off at a sharp angle.

'I expect,' she said one day over by the far flowerbeds, 'you would like to see me wee. Wouldn't you?'

I replied that I rather thought I would.

She reached out a hand and caught hold of me and we ran towards some bushy cover at the side of the hotel, away from the front windows. Then she raised her skirt with one hand and held it bunched against her stomach, and with the other hand she pushed down her panties. Crouching awkwardly, she released a brief golden stream while I took careful note of it. When she had finished she sprang up, still with her skirt raised and her panties down, and twirled around gaily.

'Well,' she said with something like regret, 'that's that.' And she began to put her clothing in order. She left the hotel a day or two later, and I did not speak to her again.

I had not seen that part of the female anatomy before and I was taken aback. I had not expected it to be like that. I wondered at the clean lines and the smooth, sculpted look of it. It seemed more elegant – more logical too – than my own little lumpy appendage. But then I thought of the palaver with the clothes, and the awkward uncomfortable squatting, and compared that with the quick action and usefulness of my own small hose, and I decided that in these particular anatomical stakes I had the best of the bargain.

*

Early in a new winter term the headmaster came looking for my brother and me. He found us upstairs, getting ready for bed. I was already in pyjamas and dressing-gown. In a friendly manner, with a hand on the shoulder, the headmaster led us into the corridor, away from the bustle of the dormitory, and while the Atlantic below the cliff grumbled and shifted, and a sharp wind jabbed at the loose panes making the black-out material over the windows catch and flutter like the luff of a sail, he told us that we were being withdrawn from the school. News had come suddenly from the War Office. The Atlantic sea-routes were now deemed safe enough for families to return to India. A passage was being arranged and we would soon be on our way.

Shivering slightly, I pulled my dressing-gown tight. What sort of news was this? Four years before, in 1940, things on the North Atlantic had not gone well for us. But my brother seemed untroubled. He was grinning and nudged me in the ribs with an elbow, as if at the start of some large piece of adventurous fun.

So we decided to take a gamble on it, to take this news more as an invitation to hope than as a cause for alarm.

★

Slowly the train worked its way north towards Glasgow. It was time for another trial by sea. The progress seemed tentative, even painful, with long sighs of escaping steam, waiting at empty country stations for clearance up the line. In the silence the boiler ticked and hissed. Windows thumped down as dim faces hung out at twilight, looking back and forth with impatience, though there was no one on the platform to question. The train was full of soldiers and we were pegged in the corridor by the crush of military bodies. Seated on a kitbag I pressed my nose against the glass of a compartment, watching warriors on their uneasy travels, smoking or trying to read in the dying light. Young faces grown up suddenly in wartime were puckered with concentration or flat with boredom. They were in the hands of the army and to struggle for any sense of dignity or individuality was pointless at the moment. Others, both in the compartments and in the corridor, were slumped in exhausted sleep. As the train got going again, heads lolled and rolled with the sway of the carriages. Arms and legs were thrown out across the passageway, or contracted into a crippled stillness. I watched these soldiers with a certain detachment. Though we were all jumbled together now, my path was not their path. We had our relief-papers in the form of a ticket to India.

In Glasgow, an ancient bus wheezed out of town to a nearby transit camp where we would stay until our ship left. All around, the Scottish winter was just beginning to grip. A dismal snowfall, not thick enough to bring to mind the pleasures of the Christmas just gone, blotched the ground and the roofs of the huts. Thin brown lines of frozen earth formed by the tramp of many feet connected the dining-hall with the outlying huts. The camp had all the sadness of decay and hasty planning. The rumour was that it had been thrown together for German prisoners in the Great War and then abandoned in peacetime. Miserably resurrected, it had all the discomfort, except the barbed wire, of a stalag.

In the hut our mother stoked the rusty iron stove with the few pieces of coke provided and we crouched close to the heat. She hung underwear and pyjamas on the fireguard and we saw the damp rise off the clothes. The uninsulated hut was raw and dank. The embrace of the sheets was slightly clammy. Curled up with coats and spare clothing piled on the blanket, I shoved my face deep into the pillow, shutting out the present and determined to dream forward to that place I already dimly knew, the place that had come into my possession through the accident of birth.

After a week or so in the camp we were taken to the docks to join our ship. This was the *Batory*, a Polish liner of dubious history that later gained some notoriety as a sort of freelance rascal of the oceans, unrestrained by either Polish communism or Western capitalism. Even as we joined it, the *Batory* appeared to be a jolly, piratical vessel, with a Polish crew taking what advantage they could from the drift of the war. Later, I thought of these sailors as the spiritual brothers of the impossibly gallant and quixotic Polish cavalrymen who (or so a well-known piece of mythology related) at the beginning of the war had charged the German panzer divisions on horseback.

The *Batory* was a passenger liner of some 8,000 tons, a well-built example of marine engineering from Gdansk, fitted out with all the mahogany, teak, rosewood and polished brass expected in the pre-war Atlantic trade. We were given a roomy cabin on the starboard side of the boat-deck, a cabin of surprising luxury. There was a large hanging cupboard smelling of pine and mothballs that one could walk into, and there were brass-handled drawers under the bunks that glided in and out with the hushed delicacy of a superior servant. The portholes, with their big brass clamps, were covered by chintz curtains that slid along a slim brass pole with knobs on the ends. Best of all, our cabin had a private bathroom, with as much hot water as we wished. It was a delicious indulgence to squander time soaking in the deep bath, watching condensation bead and drip along the bright metal and the heavy dark wood of the fittings.

I took this luxury as some recompense for unnameable wartime wrongs.

★

In memory, I have the impression that the simple step from dock to deck was the crossing of a fateful line. Snow-flecked Scotland lay along the banks of the Clyde, dirty and worn-out by war, but the low winter sun picked out our ship rising hopefully above this depressing toil. Any sea-voyage to a remote land is an entry to strange possibilities. That was something we were ready for. We wanted to emerge from shadows, to bring an end to deprivation and tears.

Almost at once I became wildly exuberant. The *Batory* had a devil-may-care air about it, and that seemed a good lead to follow. My conduct, already bad enough owing to frequent fits of temper, changed for the worse. I think it was not so much naughtiness – at least, not *extra* naughtiness – but more a lightness after a lifting of weight, a release of pressure when the valve blows.

But this was an unpleasant surprise for my mother, dragged down by four years of a lonely penury with little human friendliness. Her own liberation was put back while she faced a new spirit of rebellion, in me and in my brother also. When she tried to cut short our incessant prowling about the ship after adventure, on the grounds that it was time for bath and bed, it was more from devilish exhilaration than from rage that I pushed her fully-clothed into the hot bath water. Naturally, I howled with fright and repentance. But later I discovered that I was not so very sorry. With a new, voracious appetite, I was testing new freedom.

'Oh you boys,' my mother cried with wounded resignation, 'I don't know what to do with you. Just wait till your father gets here.'

My father's arrival was expected. For the whole war he had been stationed in the Middle East, and now it was planned that he should join our ship en route back to India. This news did not mean much to me. I had only the dimmest picture of my father, and the abstract notion of fatherhood, and what that meant to children, had no hold on my mind. Nor was the image of father as bogeyman very attractive.

For my mother, pale and slight and always on the verge of

ill-health, the anxieties of war, which for the most part had resolved into a meagre life full of hopeless compromise, gave way to the vague but abundant worries of peace, which may not have formed a torrent but flowed into a wider maze of channels under different currents. As a result, her wartime frown was displaced by the no less marked frown of peace. She took personally all the whims of chance, good and bad.

'Oh, that sun,' she would say with a baleful glance at the hot sky that promised us so much liberty, 'it always brings out my rash.'

She sat on the shady side of the boat in a long deckchair, waiting for the steward to bring the mid-morning bouillon. A scarf or a straw sunhat was arranged carefully against the glare. As the sun crossed the sky she shifted her position, sighing apologetically, 'Of course, this weather always brings me out in freckles.' As if that were a good reason for parcelling up the sun and posting it away. Whatever the sun might do for the rest of us, it had it in for her.

Her anxiety tracked us around the ship, which was a rich play-ground for a couple of energetic young lads. Polish sailors, whose English did not go much beyond a dockside lingo of sex and swearing, tolerated our games. From engine-room to bridge, we wandered more or less at will, occasionally balked by a scowl or a cuff on the ear. Sometimes, penetrating into forbidden territory, we were headed off by an irate seaman, at a loss for English words, but stamping on the iron gratings to drive us away like troublesome geese. Always hungry, we pestered the kitchen hands between meals, mooching around the service door that led into the cooks' sweaty cave. As we entered warmer seas, in all but the worst weather that door was thrown open for air. When the kitchen hands came out for a cigarette, looking sticky in stained singlets and long soiled aprons, we badgered them for titbits, enduring lively Polish oaths for the sake of a biscuit.

On fine days, after the crew had practised their drill on the gun-placements, my brother and I were sometimes allowed to take turns on the springy metal seat behind the ack-ack guns. Lifted there by callused nautical hands I gazed at the ocean skies through the spoked wheel of the gun-sight. In imagination I sent whole armadas of Dorniers and Messerschmitts spiralling into the sea. 'Rat-a-tat-tat,' I yelled in childish glee. The Poles applauded noisily. 'Blody gud show. Too many fockin German in sky.'

Our shipboard life, if we were not in the greasy realms of winches and hawsers and machinery, was spent on deck. We wanted the freedom of open air. At first, it was not so easy to get out. The Atlantic weather was wet and brisk with the wind blowing keen off the white-topped waves. The ship had a queasy motion. At these times I felt a swell of gorge in my throat and often had to make a rush for the lavatory. Choppy seas drove us down the west coast of Ireland, then we set a course away from the northern winter. We were in a loose convoy, more for administrative convenience than for safety, great grey shapes in wartime drab, merchantmen as well as sleek liners, rolling like a school of migrating whales. As the weather became milder we crossed the Bay of Biscay without sea-sickness. At the straits of Gibraltar, the passenger liners peeled off for the Mediterranean and the Suez Canal, while the merchantmen set route for the long haul round the Cape of Good Hope.

Lands went by, looking from the deck no more than lumps and shadows – the point of Tunisia, Sicily, Malta. Then we kept south, past the low dun-coloured coasts of Libya and Egypt. Throwing pieces of stale bread to the escort of gulls I saw my first dolphins, a sign, according to the Polish sailors, of the very best kind of luck. But the Mediterranean, lacking the wilder chances of the ocean, seemed a dull enough place. What was history to a child on a boat?

At Port Said, where we anchored to await the canal pilot, we were assailed by a flotilla of bum-boats. From the profuse jumble of men and goods on the wharves, the long shallow boats knifed out into the harbour with their crews of bearded hustlers already yelling a fervent sales pitch. Paddling into the lee of the ship they bawled upwards to the faces lining the high decks, offering indiscriminately things both useful and futile, with a few objects of real beauty amid the junk – rings and jewellery, etched bowls and long-necked copper jugs, pottery patterned in raw colours, glassware, small prayer rugs, carved wooden animals stylized in the manner of ancient Egypt, models of the Sphinx and the Pyramids, printed cottons and wool jellabas, framed pictures of old beast-headed gods copied from tomb-paintings. As the time passed the haggling grew more frantic. Our deckhands were laying out ropes and lounging by the winches, getting ready to ease the ship away. The opportunities were fleeting, and as the normal stock drew no more takers more intimate stuff was unveiled in a babble of many languages. With bold and hopeful gestures the vendors displayed condoms and dildos, and devices for private pleasures, and most explicit pictures of very peculiar couplings.

Then lines were dropped, the hooter blasted, and the propellers began to churn harbour muck. Yet the vendors still did not give up, but pursued with energetic strokes. As their boats fell behind, they were still waving rugs, or scarves, or shawls, or tasselled cotton robes, or pornographic wall-hangings.

Pushing my way between the legs of the adults and popping my head between the bars of the rails I could see that all this commotion was highly diverting. The passengers, whether eager to buy or not, hung over the rails with their mouths open. Nothing like this, I realized later, had erupted, so garish and blatant, into the grey disquiet of wartime England. They were shocked and glad to be so. This, after all, was the gate to the Orient about which they had certain secret expectations. So long as Western fundamentals were not completely outraged, cheeky indiscretion and mischief were permitted, under the heading of *exotica*. It was expected, even appreciated, that a journey to the East led to a loosening of the braces all round.

One after another in line astern the big ships entered the Suez Canal, as if shuffling slowly through a sea of sand. By our side, surprisingly close but far below, strings of camels often kept pace, swinging along with their tortuous gait. It looked like a new way of doing something even as old as walking. Then the ships threaded the Great Bitter Lake, members of a monstrous modern caravan, huge arks making so little stir that their wakes hardly ruffled the water.

★

When we reached Suez we stopped once more. The sunshine was bright and penetrating and the days began to get sticky before noon. In the morning the ship's makeshift cinema was showing a Laurel and Hardy film. My brother and I were keen spectators, for in wartime England we had seen very few films.

In the midst of the performance there was a sudden commotion. A dim adult figure appeared behind us, whispering, 'You two, come quickly. There's someone to see you.'

Neither of us wished to leave. My brother slumped down in his seat and grumbled over his shoulder.

'Can't it wait? Look, we're just getting to a good bit.'

Kids about us were biting their thumbs with excitement and having hiccups from laughter. But we were pulled out in a sulk. Then I saw the light flooding in through the broad open port where new passengers were making their way into the ship. I saw my mother standing just out of the eddy of the crowd, and next to her but not touching her was a tall thin man. He looked handsome to me, even though he wore the comical khaki shorts and the long woollen socks that soldiers wore in the desert. The bare knees of his long legs looked hairless and vulnerable. I noted the trim military haircut, carefully brushed with the parting almost dead centre, and on the upper lip the little clipped hedge of the moustache. He was holding a cigarette in his left hand and something else in his right.

We gazed at this man, not sure what was expected of us.

'It's your father,' said our mother in a quiet voice, sounding a bit resentful, as if we should have known him instantly.

The tall man cleared his throat. 'Hallo, boys,' he said in a voice that was embarrassed and too loud. 'How are you?'

We said nothing but stood looking hopeless. The silence seemed to knot him up with shyness. He cleared his throat again and then thrust out his right hand.

'Look,' he said more softly, having got control of his voice. 'I've brought you bananas. Take them. Please.'

PART II

IN THE CLEAR

FIVE

A Brief Introduction
to Magic

A MONG THE ACCOUNTS of the British in India, I have read that when the Jesuit Thomas Stevens, the first Englishman to write about the country, was approaching the shore of the Western Ghats in 1579 he met a succession of strange sights. First, he saw land birds he did not know far out at sea; then boughs of palms and sedges lying sodden in the water; then swimming snakes; and then 'a substance which they call by the name of a coin of money, as broad and as round as a groat, wonderfully printed and stamped of nature, like unto some coin'. After these signs, the ship's company, which was reduced to crumbs of hardtack and lacked any water, knew that a landfall was certain.

It is fitting that a counterfeit of coins was strewn along the path to India, a country so fateful for the wealth of England. Wealth is the chimera of history, waxing and waning with time. But we, arriving some 350 years later, were given no portents. Coming out of the night we strolled onto the deck in the morning and found Bombay already upon us.

To the left was the Gateway of India, a grandiose arch through which our passengers did not go.

From a distance it had a look of Marble Arch in London, and the implausibility of triumphal arches everywhere. What reason could there be to go under that particular hoop for our voyagers? It would have been a form of bowing the head, an abasement or servility not likely to be found on the Polish *Batory*. Our ship was no imperial harbinger, no collector of tribute and salaams, but only an adventurer subsisting on the broken scraps of wartime. So we shied away from the ceremonial landing, going to starboard and easing into Bombay docks.

An appalling noise greeted us. Not just the customary clang and clatter of the dockside but an overwhelming racket of people. Was it human effervescence or something more ominous? How hard it was for the English to judge. In the worst moments of the Blitz, when the heavens spat bombs and buildings burst like balloons and St Paul's was backlit by sulphurous flames, as if by the hand of Hollywood, the English went dumbly to their tasks, clutching quiet agonies to careworn breasts, celebrating escapes with wry grins and only an exhalation through the nose to show pent-up terror.

But this Indian cacophony? Even an inexperienced child had reason to see both effervescence and despair. The sun shone beautifully; the February heat was not yet overbearing; in the morning the air retained at least a memory of a breezy freshness off the Arabian Sea. On land, no sirens wailed. Coolies, barrows, rickshaws, tongas clogged the view, not vehicles in military blotches. This land was not at war. Yet there were casualties all around, with injuries as foul as war wounds. Rotted noses, blind sticky eyes, leprous skins, stumps, scars, twisted extremities. A grizzled skeleton swung himself forward at dizzy speed on rough crutches. A half-man, cut off at the thighs, propelled himself on a little wooden trolley with rag-wrapped knuckles. A bent woman pulled the edge of her sari over the earthquake of her face. Children gazed with sunken eyes as dark as mercury pools, their ribs fluttering like flimsy bamboo fences. Everything seemed in furious motion, though when the eye stopped careering about and fixed for a moment on a single person, as likely as not one saw extreme lethargy or exhaustion being dragged around like Sisyphus' stone.

*

After a while, boxed about with the bags and cases of travel, we made the first descent into the torrent of this life. Leaving Ballard Pier we could glimpse in the distance the startling architectural phantasmagoria of Victoria Terminus railway station. Going to the hotel we passed streets with surprising English names, decent avenues whose orderly colonial purpose was obscured or perverted by the rash or bloom of native enterprise. Vendors, hawkers, hustlers, beggars, loungers, the myriad homeless, all contended for space amid the press of so many thousand hurrying feet helping to make the money go round. In choked streets stenches and aromas chased each other. Garbage and sewage and stagnant water and decaying offal fought against spices and a strong flower scent and the pungent smell of cooking foods and the tang of woodsmoke. We went slowly, edging round pi dogs frantic with ticks and sores, and near-naked kids doing their ablutions in the gutter.

For a child, all these were not marks of squalor or backwardness or oppression. They were the cause of excitement – a catch in the throat. Suddenly a stubborn lock was sprung, a new door flew open, the young mind reeled with possibilities and revelations. The city was ablaze with shape and colour. A helter-skelter of crazy building – towers, spires, turrets, domes, columns, statues, balconies, porticoes – mad bits and pieces that I later knew to be Renaissance or Palladian or Gujerati or Moghul or Persian. Or, making the eye dizzy, buildings voluminously Victorian, overshadowing all the rest, as if drugging the city with the fatuous rhodomontade of empire. All this made a child's heart jump, seeing what looked like a wonderful, convoluted joke, beyond understanding but not enjoyment. The sunlight leapt from domes and windows and tiled walls. Particles of dust in the dirty air began to shimmer. We were dazzled by the assault on the senses, and then glad to hurry into the high cool lobby of the hotel.

A big fan turned lazily with a weary electric hum. A man in a tightly wound turban and a crisp white cotton tunic, in style and length rather like a frock-coat, awaited us solemnly. Suddenly his serious brown face was slashed with the brilliant white of his smile. He raised his hands to breast level in the attitude of prayer and briefly bowed his head. Then he addressed my father.

'Ah, sahib,' he said with great enthusiasm, 'I have for you jolly good rooms. On second floor, best front place, *gussul khana* adjacent. Very pleasant, tip-top view. You see this way Museum, that way University. And maidan, very green and nice. Also, you see sky, happy breeze and peaceful sleeping at nighttime.'

He clapped his hands, then with frowning dignity gave

instructions in a native tongue to a small lithe lad, hardly bigger than I was, who seemed to double as bell-boy and porter. The little fellow seized upon one of our lighter travel bags, indicating indignantly when we tried to help him that he would fetch the rest later, and though it was a struggle for him he insisted on leading the way up the stairs. As we followed up the elegant curve of the broad steps, with rusted iron banisters on our right, I puzzled over this English I had just heard, and snatches of which I had caught on the dockside and in the street. This language was mine, but not quite mine, misted and veiled with hints and shades that made me, even then, smile with surprise – not because I felt that what they said was in any way *wrong*, but because of its novelty. It seemed like an extension of English expression, nicely elastic, not an impediment.

At the head of the stairs we found that our rooms were on the first floor, not the second, and at the back, not the front. The bathroom was not 'adjacent' but a short way down the hall. My father, experienced in the ways of India, did not complain or demand changes. The rooms we were shown were tall and dim and quiet, the quieter for being at the back, away from the busy road. Ornate iron bedsteads were anchored like galleons on the green sea of the tiled floor where numdah rugs with simple, childlike designs also floated. Long louvred shutters led onto two dangerous-looking balconies. The view beyond the shutters was not airy maidan nor the great swelling dome of the Museum, but the fading yellowish wall of a house across the alleyway. Tinkles of family laughter and smells of home-cooking punctuated our days, filtering in through the louvres.

*

'Do take the boys out,' said the wan voice, as feeble and shaky as a new-born kitten, 'they're making such a *row*.'

My mother did not like the big city, with the heat and the noise, and so much evidence of the scars and sores of Indian life. Her Indian world had been, and would be again, the lazy life of the Raj in a military cantonment. And after four years in England she was finding it hard to acclimatize to the sweaty heat of Bombay. But we were stuck in the city for a week while my father awaited his orders. Nothing much to do, for any of us, morn to night. My mother went shopping, slowly, with wet patches spreading in the armpits of her frock and tendrils of fair hair growing dark with sweat at the back of her neck. She had to buy hot-weather clothes for the family, loose cotton garments and sandals and hats against the sun. Looking for good buys – it seemed to be an article of faith among the British, when shopping among Indians, that prices were to be beaten down so that every purchase became a bargain – she wandered in the maze of bazaar streets to the north of Crawford Market, taking a bearing on the golden pinnacle of the temple to the mouthless Mumba Devi, poking among the blind cubby-holes of the Bhuleshwar Market. She returned to the hotel drawn and tired, dragging her feet into the darkened room. She lay down with a damp towel over her eyes, counting the throbs of her headache.

So we left her and began the wary process of getting to know a father.

My father was not athletic – very far from it. He moved in a clumsy way – a left-hander who had not adapted to the world being the wrong way round – and he was rather lazy, having been spoilt in childhood by the clutch of women in his household. Walking, which he enjoyed, was the only concession he made to exercise, and nature had equipped him well for this. His long legs swung forward briskly, and his lean frame was not much affected by heat and humidity. So, driven forth from the hotel, we set out, the tall fellow with sleek dark hair, in well-ironed tunic shirt and trousers of razor-edge creases and soft suede shoes, tugging in his wake two rumpled boys, heated with sun and argument and exuberant energy, with pale winter skin and grimy knees and socks about the ankles.

Crossing the knife-edge of shade into the broiling street, we walked with no particular direction or purpose in mind. We seemed free and easy, but this was a complicated time. We were taking a look at India, getting re-acquainted, as it were, with a forgotten birthright. And we were trying to re-discover a family, separated for too long by war, for which absence there was some unspoken rancour against our father in our young hearts, and no doubt some sorrow and regret in his. He had some explaining to do, some persuasive gestures to make to smooth away the rough memories of the last four years. These words and gestures would not come easily.

Trained in the reticence of country folk, stamped by Methodism and poverty, he had so little practice in the language of the emotions. But he could begin by showing us around, guiding his whelps to a home territory; for my father regarded India, not England, as his home range, where he had lived most of the years beyond his youth, and had become confident in manhood and prospered and hoped to end.

But where should he begin? What a maze history leaves! Deposit after deposit, shards of strange species, evolving, enduring, then degenerating. Holding on against a current whose course is always obscure and eventually contrary. There were arguments here too labyrinthine for the tidy military mind, and of course way beyond the understanding of children. The best approach was to sample the city and let the weight of the past sink in.

We strolled down Colaba, through fashionable streets, making a circuit and returning along Apollo Bunder between city and sea. There was an unlikely familiarity in the names. Ormiston, Barrow, Henry, Walton. Who were these men (we may take it for granted that they were not women)? Now, I see sun-red faces and wigs dusted with cornflour, coarse confident visages as in a Kneller portrait. They washed in and out with the tides of time. Once, they were imperial actors, but for India, what did they intend? That was a tangled knot that history was still trying to undo. Today, their names remain, largely forgotten but still markers of a sort, alien words sounding peculiar in the mouths of local postmen.

We walked, and came upon questions not answers. Later, with luck, we would know something, or at least begin to feel something in our bones. For the moment we registered only questions. What was the meaning of that alarming fish-stink, creeping up from the southern streets as bold as an invading army? Those lofty houses in Arthur Bunder Road – they had an anomalous air. Their position shouted commerce, but the elegant, time-worn wooden tracery of their galleries suggested the sensibility of artists. Were statues in honour of Indians *permissible*? We children wondered at that. In the world we had just left, statutes represented white men – kings, politicians, generals, men with the rape of society and many capital murders under their belts – or occasionally the freaky presence of a woman. But that figure of Sivaji on a horse, he seemed to have a look of provocation that would be worrying to governors of empire.

And what lesion of the imagination had caused such bloated, disordered buildings as the Taj Mahal Hotel or, even more grotesque, Victoria Terminus station? Castles in the air, forced on by overwrought ambitions, these dreams somehow solidified into stone. Yet blasted by the city's sunrays they rose above the tumult with cockeyed gaiety. Each, in its own way, was a hive for a portion of the multitude. The rich and the up-and-coming and their fawning acolytes rustled money and peddled influence in the vast byzantine-baronial halls and bars of the Taj Mahal, while poor workers and a desperate scrum of downward-descending populace made bleak home under the aspiring squiggles and fol-de-rols of Victoria Terminus.

After a day we were tired of wading among people, so thick was the density on the streets. To feel this city, to test the texture of it, was a strenuous business. Having sweated the downtown avenues we went over to Back Bay in search of a breeze, past the cricket ground and along Marine Drive. We were heading slowly, with many stops and with help from rickshaw or tonga, for Malabar Hill, a bold city flank still with remnants of green cover, which spoke of exclusivity in this place of seared grass and the heat-palpitating daze of the streets. We no longer talked much. We children were grumpy, and our father now had the martyred air of the put-upon parent. In the jostling mob of vendors round Chowpatty Beach his temper slipped a bit, both with the crowd and with us. This urban chaos was not a soldier's India. This was the sort of uproar that civil society got itself into, a folly that soldiers could not mend. At least my father recognized that, but he was sufficiently military to regret the loss of discipline and to bridle at the liberties of the hustlers. For the Raj, however well-intentioned, when stretched and annoyed fell back on a fundamental demand for space and deference. Even the best of white men were tainted with a sense of superiority.

'Make way there,' he ordered in parade-ground manner, using his height and his elbows to lever a way through. From time to time he added something in military Urdu, bringing a flush to his own face, though it did nothing to quiet the babble pressing upon us.

But we children were transfixed by the excited, unlicensed weird-ness of it all, with hands offering us strange comforts on all sides. Our father was not pleased and turned a frosty eye on us.

'No, most certainly not,' he snapped as we clamoured for *bhel puri* or a samosa or a bhaji. 'What would your mother say? Look at the flies and the filth. And in all this heat and dust.'

The day was hot and we could have done with something wet and cold, but the *kulfi* looked as suspicious as the rest of the food. So the ice-cream was also forbidden us. My father was never subject to the sudden whims of taste. I remember a much later occasion, on a sizzling day in Italy. I had cajoled him into trying an ice-cream cone, just because I wanted one. His composed face licked the dripping cone impassively, granting me a favour rather than satisfying himself.

But for the moment, at Chowpatty Beach, he went so far as to allow us a paper twist full of peanuts.

The sea off the Beach looked greasy with spoil and the water under this film too sluggish to heave itself into waves. It crept into shore bearing an offering of queasy odours. Dusting vendors and beggars from his path with firm sweeps of his arm my father led us almost at a trot towards the Hill, seeking shade and a temporary escape from the painful asking in the faces of the hustlers. We fled into crooked ascending alleys, past the priests and the pilgrims of Balbunath Mandir, sidling around the flanks of loose wandering cows that were blocking the mêlée with the insolence of their holy state and favouring pilgrims with long doleful looks from under silken eyelashes. We mounted steps broken by weather and neglect, through steep woods to the ridge road. On the ridge, the views were very fine and the road led, with an air of inevitability, to more temples. Perhaps from this time began the feeling, which only later could I put into words, that this land was much trodden by the gods.

But my father, who had very little religious sensibility, was puzzled as to who owned what. Surely that was another Hindu shrine? No, it was a Jain temple, as neat and solemn and composed as the Jains themselves, with the shoes of the worshippers in orderly racks beside the door. But that, further down the road, was the famous Walukeshwar Mandir, where Shiva had done something bold – I believe my father mentioned the *Ramayana*, though the details of the story escaped him – and left a characteristic *lingam* as evidence of his godly potency.

My father was anxious to skirt around that topic and merely mumbled gruffly that 'we'd learn about all that soon enough'. He could not bring together the legacy of the Methodist morality of his upbringing with the unblushing sexual iconography of the Hindu gods.

Below the temple, down a rough slope, was Banganga Tank, an inviting pool despite the green scummy bloom on the water. Rama's arrow had struck out the spring that fed this pool, and thus it became a holy bathing-place for believers. On an ordinary day it was nothing much, cool and peaceful and unhealthy amid the circling tenements, a resting place for the slum-dwellers and the dhobi-wallahs of the nearby shore who washed laundry next to the burning-ghats of the dead.

After a couple of days my brother and I were done with these sticky, aggravating city marches. We slopped along in our father's trail more and more slowly, keen to get cool, to give ourselves the indulgence of a day's swimming. But even in search of a pool we could not get out of the shadow of religion. On the western shore quite close together, stood the contrasting shrines of the Muslim saint Haji Ali and of the Hindu goddess Lakshmi, Bombay's favourite deity and the provider of prosperity and beauty, both of which were needed in large measure to make a mark in the fabulous grime of this city.

From a distance, the mosque of the saint, at the end of a narrow tide-washed causeway, with elegant Moghul proportions and the bright white of its dome set against the ocean or the rusty sunset, had the advantage over Mahalakshmi Mandir, larded with the usual riot of figure and shape beloved of the Hindu religious imagination. For Westerners, that was the first and natural reaction, a view formed according to the chaste aesthetic of Greece and the reformed purity of Islamic representation. But once, after many lookings, the eye had become accustomed to the local visual dramatics, I came gradually to see that the faiths demonstrated in both monuments were, at some primitive level, not dissimilar. They were both grounded in the heartache and yearning of the battered humanity that clogged these holy places, people praying, begging, suffering, threatening, pleading, buying and selling pathetic junk in the commerce of devotion. Belief was their last refuge, whereby they gained daily breath and bread, and so tied bodies to souls. What they offered in the steamy sun of these religious precincts was not primarily merchandise or services, but a naked dearth that called forth the charity and good works without which humankind relapsed into gangs of bandits and predators.

The gods (peace be unto their many names) sprinkled temples and mosques plentifully on this land, and by doing so allowed for the exercise of humane qualities transcending the boorish pre-occupations of money, ambition, power and success. But these places were slovenly because people were slovenly. Sanctity did not negate man's mess. No matter. A place was not holy because of fine architecture, or beauty of decoration, or the silence of awe, nor on account of scrubbed courtyards and well-kept paths and mute orderly pilgrims. A place was holy because it was god-visited, nothing more. A deity that knew divine business would do well to pitch salvation down among the poor and lowly who most needed it and sought it out. Desperate people do not lead pretty lives. But it helps them to be met on their own ground by accommodating and friendly spirits.

There was, though, something jarring on first acquaintance about the intensity of the effort made by these scarecrows and skeletons to keep themselves alive secured by such slender ropes of faith and hope. I found the twisted faces, scorched eyes, spittle-flecked mouths, reaching gnarled hands put too much strain on my ignorance and timidity. I was afraid of them.

In this mood we fled, feeling unclean just through proximity, and hurried to our swim at Breach Candy. Here, among the sahibs and the native well-fed, we splashed in the waters of privilege under a sun that seemed imprisoned in geostationary orbit just over our lucky heads.

Later, in the soft evening of a day well-spent in the idle pleasures of the swimming pool, we returned satisfied to the hotel. Nearby, the strains of 'Home Sweet Home' drifted from the Rajabhai clock-tower. All was well.

★

At breakfast time, the manager of the hotel was hovering at the foot of the stairs. He looked pleased with himself, like a djinn just popped out of his bottle.

'Oh, sahib,' he cooed, trotting beside my father to the dining-room, 'today we have magic-man coming, making magic for you. Ver-ry good fun. He go upstair, about tea-time, make all family ver-ry happy.'

In late afternoon we were awaiting the magician in our rooms. He was a tall elderly man, dignified in a loosely tied snow-white turban, though his natural gravity was undermined by a big drooping moustache. His assistant followed him, carrying the props in an old suitcase coming apart at the seams and secured with several passes of a frayed rope. While we waited in one bedroom the magicians gathered themselves in the other, fussing with the apparatus, erecting a screen across a corner, changing into coats resplendent with silky colours and sparkles and cut-price jewellery. We caught fierce whispers, hissing out from below the doggy moustache, harrying the assistant. After a long interval they were ready and we hurried in with the too-eager expectation that children give to the promise of amazement.

But the magician was stern. Not for him the ingratiating joke or the casual, flip delivery. His attitude asked for attention and respect. What was being attempted was a ritual, rich and strange, a revelation of old wonders.

He held up his hands impressively, a ring on every finger, and the performance began.

Very soon, he had demonstrated that he was a master of incompetence. Not only did he have tricks up his sleeve, but it was easy to see where they were. Cards fell to the floor, transformations stalled, the coloured scarves got themselves into a hopeless tangle, the tap of the magic wand collapsed the magic box that revealed . . . well, nothing – no rabbit, no dove, no fluffy chicks. While the assistant was in a flurry, dipping in and out behind the screen, trying to make the tricks behave themselves, the magician himself went on imperturbably. When a card fell to the floor he covered it quickly with a stealthy foot. His incantations rolled out sonorously, while his long cloak swooped and soared over the rickety table of his effects.

'Why, the man's a fool,' my mother muttered beneath her breath. My mother was always anxious that promises should be kept, in life or in commerce. To her, an unmagical magician was merely a charlatan. He certainly wasn't worth good money.

'W-e-ll,' said my father with a doubtful, almost conspiratorial grin.

I could see that my father was enjoying the performance. And my brother and I were in a barely contained rapture, on our mettle to anticipate what could go wrong next.

'Look,' whispered my brother, bouncing his feet on the floor with excitement, 'he's got something hidden at the back of his collar.' And then he added with a whoop, 'No, no, it's one of the handkerchiefs that should be in the hat!'

I was in such excruciating pleasure that I had to cross my legs and squeeze them tight, for fear of disgracing myself with a little puddle under my chair.

The magician, feeling a lack of proper solemnity and mystery, brought the performance to an abrupt end. But he did not lose his dignity. A deep salaam, a tug at his ragged moustache, and he retired behind the screen in good order, leaving his assistant to scoop up the malfunctioning props.

After a while two shadows slipped from the bedroom, the long elderly one holding a black rolled umbrella like a staff, and the smaller one lopsided under the weight of a bulging wrecked suitcase.

★

Abbé Dubois, the inquisitive French missionary who spent thirty-one years in the Madras Presidency obscuring his priesthood under a brahmin's robes, in the wonderfully detailed anthropological investigations that he had compiled by 1823, had many things to say about magicians. They were highly respected and feared in Hindu society, though their trade was dangerous, threatened by the jealousy of the spirits, the rebounding of spells, the revenges of rivals, the obduracy of gross material objects.

But their powers were satisfactory for even the most wild-eyed egomaniac. Brahma, Vishnu, Shiva – the great gods themselves – could not resist the magicians. These men plied their occult trade with the planets and elements in tow, aided by ghosts, earth devils, malign female *sakti* spirits, and death-dealing Kali, goddess of destruction. The Abbé, who showed a nice line in ironic appreciation, had a soft spot for these wonder-workers. He mentions a master who mixed the bones of sixty-four different living beings – a man born on the Sunday of the new moon, a woman born on Friday, bones from the feet of a cobbler, a pariah, a Muslim, a Ferangi, and many others – then buried the mess under propitious stars at the threshold of an enemy and infallibly caused that enemy's death. Another magus, muttering a mantra such as *h'hom, h'rhum, sh'rhum, sho'rhim, ramaya, namaha*, whose effects were decisive and irresistible, mixed the mud of sixty-four filthy places (sixty-four and its factors seemed to be the efficacious numbers). He worked in human hair, nail clippings, bits of human dross, and moulded it all into figurines, each with the name of an enemy on the breast. Then, if the incantations had been scrupulously followed, those persons were done for. The *grahas*, the planetary influences, took hold of them and led them a merry dance to perdition.

Thirty-two weapons, licked by the blood of human sacrifice, could put a besieging army to flight, making a huddle of defenders look like a battalion of thousands. The roots of sixty-four noxious plants, prepared with spells, could make a secret hash of the life of any hated rival.

From this treacherous and resplendent world, time and Western conquest led India into the twentieth century. Now rationalism bites, materialism begins to sweep the intellectual ground, agnostics trample over belief. Something is gained in the direction of sobriety and good sense. But something, the wilder poetry of instinct and wonder, is lost too, or debased into a maladroit sideshow for cocky Western children.

SIX

The Vindhyas

LAND OF TRAINS, bearers of modernity and restlessness.
It was not hard to leave Bombay. After a short while the
city began to frighten us. People bent low under their burden
of calamity and desperation – bleeding lives, emotions worn to the
nub, the immensity of the hopelessness. We children wanted sun
without this painful stink of sweat, space where we would not be
elbowed by the agonies of others. With relief, we put Victoria
Terminus behind us, for though we did not know it then, that
bloated architecture was the emblem of our disappointments.

Invented grandeur is one of many imperial failings. It mocks what
it strives to assert. The boasts become jokes: a lion on one side of the
entrance, a tiger on the other; a figure of Progress, twelve foot tall,
surmounting the dome of the building; predatory animals carved in
the crannies of the vast space, watching below with bleak stone eyes.
The Victoria Terminus was the proclamation of a deliberate pro-
gramme for India. It was planned as the high temple for a land
transfigured by the British introduction of Western commerce and
industry. These were the new recruits for the ancient Indian
devotion to the god of the paisa. And here in the station precinct, in
a murky ambience of steam and smoke, a servant of that god – the
Great Indian Peninsular Railway – with much whistling and metallic
thunder began to take us off into the folds of central India, into a
land beginning to lack ancient heart, and as yet without a full
confidence in the new.

The days were hot, working up to the full ferocity of the high
summer months. In the carriage my brother and I jostled to get by a
window, welcoming the small gale of dust and soot-laden air

blowing through the rattling frames. After jolting slowly through the
human driftlands of the city's edge the train assumed a leisurely pace
into a countryside that gradually emptied itself of people. Where had
they all gone? A population so brazenly, so appallingly, present in
Bombay seemed to recede from sight. Lonely figures became lost in
landscape, bled out by harsh sunlight into a world of shadows.

Recalling that journey now, I see stasis rather than movement:
peasants on dusty paths like representations on a frieze, the slow train
losing them from sight between one step and another; an old man at
rest, naked but for a loincloth and a baggy turban, stretching his
bones on the twisted ropes of a *charpoy* bed; gaunt dogs lying still
enough to mimic death; cattle with their heads down, defeated by
the pestilence of flies; a solitary buffalo knee-deep in a pool at whose
edge a solitary woman straightened and held her back beside a pile
of washing. Here and there smoke arose out of the trees in thin
pillars, drifting up towards zones of bleached air where kites, hardly
moving, smoothed the sky with their great wings.

Places without motion abolish time. Was that the deception
practised by rural India? Each snapshot through history looked very
much like the one before it. A row of small monkeys sitting on the
roof of a wayside station, grimacing like wicked senators, might
have been from the age of Ashoka. Weather and nature embraced
the buildings of all ages, returning them to the equal status of the
semi-ruined. Only the train seemed to provide the connecting
thread of a narrative. But what was the story it told? From green
hills freckled with jungle we descended into broad valleys, then
clattered gingerly on bridges of rusting girders over wide rivers that
were nameless to me, before labouring into the next range. This
long rocking rhythm up and down was like counting the ribs of a
somnolent land. Then, by the tracks, suddenly a large town would
swell out of the trampled dirt, tilting towards chaos, with people
congealed together like flies on a fly-paper. The stasis broke apart.
An inhospitable present rubbed a filthy nose along the windows of
the carriage.

The train crossed the Narmada river and climbed slowly into the
Vindhya hills. Dregs of mist still clung about the deeper places.
White water rushed in ravines, bellowing into caverns. Clouds piled

on the ridges and the escarpments above vegetation lush with the juice of good rainfall.

At the southern edge of the Malwa plateau, not far from Indore, the train let us off at the little town of Mhow. This was a cantonment of the Raj, founded in the early nineteenth century with a keen eye for geographical position, administrative convenience, and the comfort of white folk sweating copiously and far from home. At the pleasant height of about two thousand feet, on a ridge falling away spectacularly to south and east, tangled in greenery, Mhow laid a cooling hand on the brow of an alien and lonely soldiery.

★

Suddenly, I almost lost sight of my parents. In the fear and loneliness of wartime England I had clung to a parental hand and was miserable when chance and time tore that hand away. Now, in this bird-singing immensity of warm morning sunshine, guidance was a restraint, and safety became a form of bondage. 'For goodness' sake,' I complained, dodging out of reach of the comb and spilling out of the door too fast for instruction to catch me.

Cheerfully tousled, my brother and I hurried to breakfast. Tables were laid on a wide verandah overlooking a large garden, which looked unkempt but was merely giving way to the profusion of nature. Wide-spreading trees, tough bushes intent on reaching the light, unknown flowers blowsy with colour, unknown birds giddy with song. The clean green was made richer by the morning sunlight before the full onslaught of the heat. Against this immoderate nature the verandah proclaimed the decent orderliness of man. Stiff white tablecloths laid with bright arrays of highly polished cutlery. Chinaware sparkling with anticipation, jugs and pots poised and ready. In the shadow of the doorways the Indian servants waited crisp in white, looking formal yet willing, eager to pad softly forward on bare feet, a murmured salaam on the lips and a big silver-plated pot of tea in hand.

Even at breakfast I was ravenous, as if physical hunger were only a part of the hunger of ignorance, an overwhelming greediness to devour a new world.

'Hallo, what's this then?' I wanted to know, plunging a spoon into the perfumed pulp of an unknown fruit.

It was papaya. At other times there was guava, or melon, or mango, or pomegranate. They were all a surprise, all wonderful. After the lean years in England I looked joyfully at the special circumstance of life that laid them in my way. How generous was this India!

★

As yet, there was no obvious purpose to our days. I know now that my father was in an administrative limbo, an incomplete line in one of wartime's muddled ledgers. Soon he would move on, but in the meantime we did not go to school. Other children went by in small groups, some with a suspicious convent-look about their uniforms. Larger boys from the Parsi school batted paper balls with ruler and scuffled by the roadside, trying to steal pencil-boxes from the girls. But we were going to the swimming pool. The tang of damp laterite, fresh from a dawn shower, was in our nostrils, and to us this was the delicious smell of freedom.

The pool was in the open air, small but clean and well-kept, set in bushy scrub but with a wide concrete perimeter. To whom it belonged I do not know, but in the times we went there no other swimmers appeared. Occasionally, young Indian boys, in long white shirts, veered off the path and stopped, chewing the ends of sticks. We didn't know enough to invite them in. They observed us carefully, half hidden by the bushes. Their brown eyes had the patient watchfulness of deer. There was no judgement in their looks. What was happening was normal. But we needed no invitation. When the unruffled blue of the pool came into view at the end of the path we ran the last hundred yards, popping buttons and flinging off clothes over our swimsuits, then jumped with abandon and smacked our pale bodies into the shallow end.

Since neither I nor my brother could swim, our father came along to keep an eye on us, though it is my suspicion that he couldn't swim either. A poor agricultural lad from the doughy earth of Lincolnshire, what would he know of waterside frolics? He held in contempt what we might now call the fashions of the Costa del Sol – the witless vanity of the beach, the painfully endured rawness of sunburnt flesh, the vacancy of idle minds. I never saw him wear a swimsuit or take off his shirt in public. Sometimes, in what for him was an act of abandon, he would roll his trousers up to the knees, though only in private moments, for he then revealed the large angry scar left on his shin by a desert sore. He was not ashamed of this disfigurement but considered it an indelicacy to expose it to the wide world.

Though I could not swim, I was experimenting. It was my notion that swimming under water was easier than swimming on the surface. If I walked slowly along the bottom from the shallow end, holding my breath, I would get the feel of being below water and lose some of the terror of sinking. Looking up, I saw the material world wobbling out of shape, refracted by the water. The shimmering pattern of the surface, seen from below, was a beautiful and unexpected reordering of the familiar universe, a liquid kaleidoscope without the sharp edges of reality. As my breath gave out I bobbed upward, clutching the rim of the pool. My head burst through the surface in a corona of bubbles, quitting the shifting translucent netherworld for the steady lines and angles of normality. I would look at my father to see if he were noticing these brilliant effects. But it would have taken a small seismic upheaval to divert him from his book. He had a deckchair arranged in a rather upright position, pulled well back from the splashes of the pool. He did not wear a hat, though the sun was hot. His dark brown hair was as neatly trimmed and parted as usual. He crossed his long legs and serenely turned another page. He did not glance up but his left hand took the ever-present cigarette to his lips.

★

Hurrying to the swimming pool one sticky afternoon I saw my mother walking a little distance ahead. I do not know where she was going but she looked fresh and calm, in a summery way. But what arrested me, I think, was her smile. Usually, my mother had more shadow than sunlight in her face. We stopped, and both of us seemed to be surprised. I felt I wanted to say something, but what that was I could not grasp. At the same time I knew I wanted to get to the pool as soon as possible, so I ducked my head and turned and ran, shouting 'Come on' to my brother in a louder voice than necessary. As I turned away I noticed that my mother was still smiling.

★

In this new place, from time to time England still came to mind. But I found it hard to recall so many days gone blank through misery. They had seemed to die so slowly, limping into the twilight gloom of the northern climate. But now, in the book of our days, the pages flicked by. It was a narrative cut with the speed and economy of a thrilling film. Too quickly, the tropical night slammed the day shut, leaving us breathless and eager for the next act.

At night, to overcome our restless nerves, our father read us long stories. I think this was the only part of parental duty that he really liked. He was a great reader himself, and a large part of his success in an unlikely profession was due to a certain bookish intelligence. Reading to us was what he did naturally and vindicated, in a small way, his general culture. He liked to expend on us some of those treasures of the mind that had so little value in the ordinary Anglo-Indian social world.

He read with great fluency, even stylishly, but without much dramatic force. He was too shy for that.

'This, O Best Beloved,' he would begin, 'is another story of the High and Far-Off Times.'

I settled down in bed, pulling the sheet up to the nose, for this was what I wanted to hear. Beguiled, I followed Kipling into that world he knew better than most, the childhood world of Wonder and Hope.

In this way, with unconscious cunning, my father directed my imagination. He put me in the world-shaping hands of Rudyard Kipling, the best guide a Western child ever had into the huge complexity of India and into the minds of India's strange historical antagonists, the people of the Raj.

Start at the beginning, said Kipling, and so I did. From my father's voice I heard of the Camel's Hump, and of the Skin of the Rhinoceros, and of the Leopard and his Spots, and of the Elephant's Child, and of Old Man Kangaroo. I became familiar with the lone walking Cat and the Stamping Butterfly. Yes, I thought, hugging my bedclothes, all this is possible in Mhow, here in India. A jungle began beyond the thin walls of our bungalow, not so very far away. In the night, wild notes swelled and died, something between warning and welcoming. It could be Mowgli out there. Now I too was in some imaginative sense a child of the forest. Coming from cities I had so much to learn, though of course I was far too frightened to think of getting to know those wise and dangerous animals of *The Jungle Book*. It was enough for me to begin to make a general acquaintance with nature. Already, in our walks to the pool, I had seen a long snake slide from the path. I was far enough away not to panic, but I was amazed to see a bare-footed Indian pass by the snake respectfully but with a certain nonchalance. The notion was still strange to me, that the deadly beast and I inhabited the same patch of earth. There was no necessity for war between us. I was learning, but I was not quite ready to say 'hallo' to the snake.

Later, Kipling would take me further, helping to lead the child-in-nature onwards towards a position of moral responsibility, helping that child become a boy-in-society, in the special society of the Indian Raj.

But for the moment all I could hear was my father saying, in a forthright military manner, 'Hear and attend and listen; for this befell and behappened and became and was, O Best Beloved.'

And so I *did* attend, though getting muggy with sleep, until my mind was awash with words, and the rhythm of them was rocking me into a land of contentment, and the last thing I heard was the now-softened voice of my father saying, 'So they went away and lived happily ever afterward, Best Beloved. That is all.'

SEVEN

A Hush in the Hostel

TO POSSESS TWO parents was new and strange to me. We had managed with less – my brother and I – in time of war. What were the rites appropriate to this new situation, this sudden addition of an extra to our settled group? What were the uses of a father? I looked at the two of them together – my parents. Though there was nothing wrong with them, I thought there was something disproportionate in their conjunction, something lopsided. And, physically, they did make an awkward pair. My father was tall and thin, cutting a dash in his clothes but a clumsy mover in well-shined shoes surprisingly small for such a tall man. A tendency to talk too loud, a pedant in small matters, a cheerful conversationalist in the Officers' Mess (joking and joshing with his fellows, those silly buggers from English public schools), an admirer of regimental tradition, a man's man. My mother was short, nervous, given to headaches. Her slimness was fashionable and lent her a stylish air which she cultivated. I remember puffy sleeves on her light cotton dresses, nipped in at the waist, and necklines cut low in a broad V. Heat brought her out in a rash, sunlight encouraged her freckles. Paleness and fair hair were a distinction for ladies in Anglo-Indian society, but they had a price. Yet her frailty seemed to call for respect and tenderness. Her movements were quick, agitated and anxious. She frowned often. She was suspicious of strangers, and doubly suspicious of most men who still appeared to her, in some secret convent-formed enclave of a peasant heart, as dirty beasts.

I watched them walking together, he still smoking, stepping out in long strides. In a while she would lag behind, beginning to droop, fanning herself with a hand. 'There's no hurry,' she would say with exasperation. And usually there wasn't. But he couldn't help himself. He drove ahead, not listening, keen to get at the root of things, convinced that the inevitable small aggravations of the Indian day would succumb to reason and good sense. He was courteous to the Indians he came into contact with – servants, clerks, box-wallahs in the bazaar and tonga-drivers – leaning down stiffly from his height to give them his whole attention. He was considerate to junior officers (specially if they were Indian), making sure all his orders were clear and simple, in words of few syllables. He always had a care for the English language and gave me at an early age a copy of *Plain Words* by Ernest Gowers.

But when things went wrong – and how easy it was, in the peculiar relationship between English and Indian, for promise to outrun performance and for small everyday events to fall into misunderstanding, indignity and foolishness – he would begin to enunciate in a voice much too loud, with heavy emphasis, as if to the slightly deaf, determined to save the day by some indisputable logic. Then my mother would grow impatient, tapping her fingers on her bag, looking away with a haughty stare, refusing to meet some plausible but unconvincing babu eye. 'Oh, come along,' she would say to my father before adding one of her favourite condemnations, 'the man's obviously a fool.'

Then my father would look at her as if he did not understand. He grew red and flustered, and his voice that had been so sensible took on a hurt, hectoring tone. So there they stood: my righteous father faced by what he thought was impudence but was more likely to be the panic of incomprehension; and the victim of his coldness hopelessly tangled in the historical thickets of racial dominance and subservience. The words were clear enough, but the two psychologies were out of step. In the end, often it was left to my mother to sort out the awkward moments. With her low expectation of strangers she did not hesitate to dazzle them with a forced charm.

'There, you see?' she would say, her triumph tinged with contempt. 'It wasn't so difficult.'

My father sulked.

★

The slow trunk road went from Mhow to Ambala. It etched a dust-obscured path on to the north Indian plain, a blind unsteady line along which the bullock-carts swayed with a soporific motion as they receded into the heat mirage lying over the baked land. A lifetime of weariness went into the pedalling of the bicyclists.

The history of India is a story of climate, though the academic books, besotted with politics and power, don't mention it much. The first Moghul emperor, Babur, that most appealing of conquerors, mentioned it. In fact, he grumbled about it a good deal. In northern India those months of high summer, Gemini and Taurus – the blazing dog-days of Jeth and Asarh – made a hell of life, throwing evil humours over the most sanguine temperaments. In this mood Babur found little good in the towns or the countryside of Hindustan. A flat, bleak, ugly, barren landscape strangled with thorny brushwood. The people were a scurrying multitude, small wretched men and women inhabiting wretched hovels of lath, mud and straw, without gardens, without water-courses, without pleasure-grounds, without graces. A land and populace beaten down under the sun. In this blistered country, the Timurid chieftain Babur might well show some misery, born as he was beneath the snowline of the Pamirs and inheriting a Persian longing for gardens and running water and ice-cold sherbet. As long as the Moghuls reigned they tried hard to repair the appalling deficiencies of a truly Hindu dearth.

But the experience of the Moghul conquerors, wistful for high green valleys and remembered snows, was also the thousand-year-old experience of the native Aryans themselves. Nirad Chaudhuri, that impish observer, even-handed praiser and abuser of all things Indian, quotes a poem said to be by the great Sanskrit poet Kalidasa. The poet speaks of the blinding whirlwinds of dust blown off the bone-dry land; of the thirst-maddened deer that takes the shimmering blue horizon for the glint of water; of the snake, writhing on ground too hot to touch, that creeps into the shadow of the enemy peacock's tail, and the frog that looks for relief under the hood of the cobra.

In the time of the Raj, the suffering English, sweating resolutely, scrambled for their hill stations.

One of those hill stations is pictured in the old photo album that I claimed after my father's death. Kasauli, site of the Indian Army

Signalling School, was in the north of Ambala District, where the
land began to hump and lean towards the Simla Hills. It was not
much of a place. The imperial gazetteer called it the least esteemed
of the Punjab hill stations 'owing to its moderate height and nearness
to the dust of the plains' . The camera, drawn back to catch the
sweep of the land around Kasauli, shows a long, sharp, precipitous
ridge, the upper third of it heavily forested, with the scattered
buildings and barracks of the small town clinging to hillside amid the
dark foliage of the firs and the *chil* pines of the sub-Himalayan flora.
Below this forest, not far from the summit, the bare, grey-brown,
scarred, scuffed tumble of rock and dirt has all the comfort of a
moonscape.

Looking now at those photos of Kasauli I see how much heartache
and nostalgia were invested in the Indian exile of the Raj. The
pictures show a re-invented topography drawn out of the memories
of a lost northern childhood. Those decent four-square bungalows
set in little fenced-in gardens; those tall brick chimneys steepling out
of tiled roofs; those paths of beaten earth, so neatly swept, protected
from the ravine beyond by stout posts and a linked chain. At the top
of the town stands the church, with a long high nave and a square
Norman tower at the west end. The barrack-blocks around the
parade ground are like large roomy barns with elegant, round
windows in the gable-ends. In the square a game of cricket goes on.
The players are in regulation whites with white floppy hats, and the
umpires are correctly dressed in long white coats. The batsman leans
forward easily in an accustomed stance, the keeper crouches close to
the wicket, the bowler has begun his run. The hands of the church
clock are poised to move. In the big bungalow of the Officers' Mess,
set amid overpowering bougainvillaea, the mess servants in tight
buttoned jackets and white turbans await. There will be beer and
pints of shandy for the first imperious thirst of the evening, and then
sherry or chota pegs of whisky before dinner.

All this claimed a little space for memory in a harsh and alien
wilderness. Beyond the small confines of the town India repossessed
its long, long history. To the north, crumpled broken land, ridge
after ridge, piled up against the distant rampart of the Himalayas. To
the south, a thin haze or a few loose clouds drifted off the hills before

dissolving into the heat-crazed torpor of a plain that appeared to have no limit.

★

Even in the photos of this old album I can see that the imposition of the Raj, under the lens of time, was a moment out of history. A turning aside. It could not last, it was an anomaly. India lapped at it, and washed over it, and submerged it for ever, like a lost city obliterated by an inevitable rise of the waters. But it retains the mystery and eerie seductiveness of lost cities, a forlorn piece of the archaeology of the human spirit, grandly – triumphantly – *wrong* in the wrong place.

Surely, among the criticisms and excuses for their conduct, we can smile at a people who made such an unforeseen, wholehearted and dedicated mistake.

★

The climate did not worry me. Why would it? The craving for adventure overcame the small burden of heat. I saw the door open dawn to dusk. Outside was a new playground called India, for a child a place of unimaginable peculiarities and riches.

Once more, we had come in transit, to this new place. Ambala, one of the largest cantonments in northern India, was placed at the point where two railways intersected with the Grand Trunk Road. It was a marshalling yard for military men. Soldiers of all kinds languished uneasily under a bitter sun, ready to move on, their fate a brief instruction in Orderly Room files awaiting the notice of clerks overwhelmed by the end of war. A time of anxious possibilities, for who knew what was the future for British India?

The native city of Ambala was a few miles to the north of the cantonment, a big teeming place, low-built, gritty, ill-favoured. There was no reason for us to go there, and I can remember only one visit. We boys went with our father, in a staff car. Father was irritable and preoccupied with military matters. Or was it the heat and the relentless dust? The town was as fretful as my father – busy, overwrought, sweaty. It appeared to be an important centre for industry and commerce. Some factories of desolate ugliness polluted the air, smoky grime falling onto red dust. The town looked confusing and the underlying order of its day-to-day life easily escaped me. Borders seemed arbitrary – between street life and shop life and home life, between trade and domesticity. Cotton garments and *kelims* in sombre colours – dusty reds and dark jungle greens – spilled out of doors and were hawked in the streets. Shopkeepers in little hidey-holes squatted on mats, reading Hindi papers or taking tea in small metal bowls. Here and there a hookah was drawing peacefully. Vendors of sweetmeats, delicacies, *pan*, cool drinks did brisk business, as if the town was too busy to cook and the vendors were the officers of some huge communal kitchen. Boys sitting behind open sacks of grain and piles of vegetables had their heads down over books of homework. The air was brushed with strange odours of spices, like a window suddenly thrown up on a room of ancient vices.

Food was much in evidence but people were thin. All around were sunken cheeks, faces drawn and creased beyond their years, arms and legs looking too fragile for their daily duties. Food, even when plentiful, was not taken for granted. The system, such as it was, that tied agricultural production to income and life was so precarious that it wavered continually about the point of collapse.

Later, in my readings about India, I thought of those pinched faces of Ambala and the swollen bellies on the stick-like bodies of the children when I read of famines in that part of the Punjab in 1860–1, in 1868–9, in 1884–5, in 1890, in 1896–7, in 1899–1900, and so on miserably into the next century. I hardly understood what was happening until I came across the pages of Amartya Sen, that famous and humane economist, who at the time I am writing about in Ambala was himself a child in the devastating famine of West Bengal. There was grain enough then (India is a fecund mother, though wilful and unpredictable), and it was stored ready for use. But after the hard times partly caused by the war the large rural population of Bengal had no income left to buy the grain, and so families must starve. There was not a lack of food but a lack of buying power. As in Ireland in the time of the Potato Famine, it was deemed better that miserable indigents should perish than that the iron laws of capitalist relations should be broken. What happened was considered inevitable. However kindly, well-informed people – economically *mature* – knew better than to monkey with the market.

There was no shortage of food for us, but we did not eat well. The quarters for the families of transient officers in Ambala – in a hostel of a sort – were gloomy places, a square blocky building marooned in a well-stamped compound of bare ground. Rooms were tall and ill-lit (keep the heat out at all costs!), the light growing dim in upper corners that needed whitewash. The old paint on the shutters was sun-blistered and flaking. Senile fans, joined to the electricity supply by frayed wires, creaked around hardly able to disturb the tepid air. The servants and the cleaners, looking unconscionably elderly, padded the quiet public rooms and the corridors, weariness falling from them like dross. The whole place was suffused with an undefeatable lassitude.

The mournful dining room unnerved even us children. Our usual hearty appetites had deserted us; we pushed the food around on the plates. Mulligatawny soup was the sole triumph of the kitchen. After that, the cook fell back, as if imagination was exhausted, to soups of the Brown Windsor variety, lumps of gristly meat in swamps of *bhindi* or brinjal, drowned potatoes, followed by sweetish custardy things of a yellow hue. Outside the hostel I had seen peasants and coolies taking a midday break on their heels in the shady lee of a wall, eating interesting messes from a battered tin plate, scooping up rice and lentils, folding chapatis around cumin- or turmeric-tinged vegetables. After a time I asked my father why we could not try what even the lowest-placed servant enjoyed. My father viewed without enthusiasm the prospect of an Indian diet. In matters of food, though he was not fussy, his tastes inclined to the pork, sausage, and pie-laden ideal of his pig-keeping Lincolnshire childhood. But he explained to me that orders had been handed down from the highest source in Delhi that British officers were not to use the standard foods of the Indian troops. Rice and chapati, in particular, were not to be eaten.

This was only a sympathetic gesture, showing consideration for a populace teetering as ever on the brink of famine. For good as well as bad reasons, what was Indian was not owed to the British, and vice-versa. Now, more than ever, it was a puzzle to know where we stood.

My father left the hostel early. Before breakfast, he roused us, coming into the bedroom I shared with my brother without ceremony. A loud 'Now, boys, up you get' squeezed the last sweet drops of sleep out of us, and then he was gone, a smart lanky figure in long socks and roomy military shorts, drawing on a cigarette as he strode into the oven of another Punjab day. Like a ship running before a brisk wind he scudded beyond our horizon and was temporarily lost to us. I did not know where he went or what he did.

Abandoned at breakfast, we also were in a sense lost. The door to the roadway was open, to catch the slightest breeze. Strong slanting sunlight lanced through the haze of dust in the broad military highway outside. Sepoys on errands went by, looking bright but not so eager that they worked up a lather. Then an infantry platoon might come flying along, stepping out with a swing under an NCO's unforgiving eye. All that world was ours to make what we could of it, doing as much each day as our invention and the merciful patience of India would allow.

'Where's Ma?' I would ask my brother, reaching for another piece of cold toast in the Victorian gilt toastrack.

Yet again she had not been seen this early in the day. We did not need her, but it was as well to keep tabs on her whereabouts. She had not left my parents' bedroom.

Soon after midday we took lunch almost on the run, in and out, unwashed and with dishevelled clothes, hardly daring to leave the scenes of the street – a donkey that kicked over a farmer's cart, a dog maddened by heat and insects growling and tearing at its own rump, a line of women in saris carrying road-chips in head-baskets, a lorry-load of jolly soldiers giving us an impromptu and ironic salute. We begrudged the time away. This was better theatre than we had ever seen in England. Still munching we ran from the bare spaces of the hostel, away from dull echoes, and the slow tap of time passing.

Sometimes, as we fled from lunch, we would see Father returning for a short afternoon siesta. I still did not know him very well but it struck me that he often looked pulled down, walking with something less than his usual spring. He looked solemn, waving only a perfunctory salute at passing soldiers. Tucking his hat under his arm he made straight for his bedroom, shutting the door carefully behind him as if some delicate tracery of sound or structure might get broken.

At some later time, going by my parents' door, I heard noises that made me stop. Something deep and confused was happening in there. I heard a rumble like stones in a heavy wooden box interspersed with bursts of rapid monotone pitching up towards the edge of hysteria or tears. Then a silence, too deep and too long. I wanted to knock but stopped my hand and went quickly away on tiptoe.

'What's the matter with them?' I asked my brother. 'Do you think they're *ill*?'

My brother didn't know. 'Well, it's hot, isn't it?' he suggested. Adults had peculiar metabolisms that left them victims to things we took in our stride. Besides, it was not our place to enquire. It was as much as we could do to make daily sense of the street-world outside. If there were something wrong close to home we would be told in good time. Instinctively, we turned from the threat of gloom. Slamming out of the hostel we rushed into the early evening where we could hear a regimental pipe band limbering up by the maidan with rapturous squeals.

My mother did not go out much. Perhaps the hostel was the coolest place, and in any case there was little she wanted to do in the cantonment. I would see her, still in her slippers, slumped in a big cane chair under the laborious fan, listlessly turning the pages of a long out-of-date *Illustrated London News*. When she came to the dining room she would hardly eat, pushing the dish aside with a wrinkling of the nose.

'Oh this *heat*,' she sighed, starting to rise then sinking back in a lump on her chair. In a while she headed back to her bedroom.

'There you are,' she would say in surprise when our paths crossed. 'Are you all right?' She looked at us quizzically, as if there were things she was struggling to understand, but she was not listening for an answer. Absentmindedly, she would put out a hand to smooth our hair or straighten our clothes. 'Just look at you,' she sighed again, 'such a mess.' Offended by a dirty nose she would make a pass at one of us with her hanky, but we were off and away before her hand could fall on us.

Then we hardly saw her at all – a back disappearing behind a door, a head bowed over sewing or sock-darning, a silent profile turned away from her husband, a pale face waiting for our perfunctory goodnight kiss. Sometimes, looking up at a slight noise and expecting to see her, I discovered only an ancient servant shuffling the floor in heelless slippers with toes turned up like the prow of a boat.

My father's face was becoming tight and stubborn. He parted and combed his dark hair with extreme care and his moustache was rigorously clipped. I was not anxious to be kissed by him, a reluctance that relieved both of us from a burdensome display of affection. We children hardly saw him, a state of affairs that seemed to suit us all. Conscientiously, he gave us our orders, as he would to his staff, and from time to time he came down on us hard for our rowdy and quarrelsome behaviour. That was as far as he wanted to go. He did not know, at the best of times, how to speak to children. Finding himself unavoidably in our company he would clear his throat, as if ready to make a general proposition on the weather or the state of the day, but then his voice would stall. He was saved by the routine of lighting another cigarette, or calling for another beer. Before picking up his book he would enquire politely, 'Anything you boys want? Another squash? No? Well, run along then till supper time. Don't be late. You know your mother expects you home.'

In a while long steps took him to his bedroom door. He reached slowly for the handle and opened the door a notch, saying quietly and apologetically, 'It's only me, dear.' A little click covered the finality of his retreat. Silence.

'Perhaps they're *both* ill,' said my brother.

*

'I still can't understand why he did that to me,' my mother said rancorously, some years after my father's death.

I was sitting with her in her little flat, under the eaves in her block of sheltered housing apartments. She had come to rest here; her own death was not far off.

In thickening winter light the great swell of the bells had just finished flooding into the room from the tower of Wells Cathedral. It was a moment for confidences. Nervously she pulled her spectacles on and off, impatiently discarding one pair of glasses, then rubbing at the smeared lens of another pair which was equally unsatisfactory. Her rheumy eye gazed over the winter muck of the farmyard next door and rested without pleasure on the saturated Mendip hills beyond. She was not reconciled to her memories.

'What had I done to deserve it?' she complained. 'There I was in wartime England, alone for four years, scrimping and saving, worried to death by you two children – you were often little devils, you know – though of course it wasn't your fault, you poor dears. And there he was, having the time of his life – he told me so – playing soldiers in Alexandria, Cairo, Beirut, Baghdad, Basra, northern Persia. No fighting, he never saw a shot fired in anger. It seemed really like one long round of pleasure, and then I think what I was going through.'

A jolly, soldier's life, sunny days, drinks in the bar of Shepheard's Hotel, a sympathetic ear from convenient young ladies (best to pass quickly over that bit), meals on the terrace of Lebanese restaurants by the gun-metal waters of the Mediterranean. Then purposeful plans to give some spice to the administrative day, a preparedness without any real danger, but still camping under stars ('when sleeping on the ground,' my father said sagely, 'always dig a little pit for your hip'). Then dozing on long night drives without lights under the amazing blaze of the desert heavens, the endless divisional columns rumbling like a distant earth tremor. Not needed for the 8th Army push in North Africa but sidetracked into cloak-and-dagger operations beyond the line of the Atrak river, towards Ashkhabad, helping Uncle Sam supply a depleted Russian army, the Yanks refusing to stir from their base-camp until the generator for their refrigerators was in place and the Coca-Cola well-cooled. Exciting games for big boys, and no one hurt. Rapid promotion too.

'Oh, why did he treat me like that?' my mother wailed, pain half a century old still in her voice. 'On that journey back to India, when I met him on the ship I was so full of joy. Life could begin once more, he and I and you two boys, whom he did not know, together in India. I wanted it to be just the way it was before the war. Then he told me in Ambala, where I was not very well anyway, that he had put himself forward for the last of the fighting in Burma. It was with those Chindit ruffians, or whatever they were called, the final push against the Japanese. We had only been together for a few months and he was happy to abandon me again!'

He could not admit it but as a soldier he felt unfulfilled, and in truth a little ashamed also. He was a professional with twenty years' service and he had seen no enemy action. It was not a case of heroism but almost a dereliction of duty. When he was sunning himself in the desert he knew only too well that many poor conscripts, reluctant and fearful warriors, had their laggard steps wiped out by death. War is a drug to some, a test to others. Under either case, however you looked at it, my father felt he had not had the advantage of the time. He wanted to know what he might do when the adrenalin rushed, and the spiteful bullets snickered about his ears, and the big demented shells plastered earth and gore on the living and dead, and the unwary suddenly plunged terrified faces into any patch of stones or litter only to discover later that they had soiled their breeches.

Sleepy India was all very well, and there were easy satisfactions to be gained in peacetime soldiering. But a flying moment, which appeared suddenly of overwhelming importance, was waiting to be grabbed. Now or never. My father wondered if a woman – a family – had the right to stand between himself and this moment of self-revelation, a last chance to test himself to the farthest depths of his professional being, his manhood. It seemed to him to be a reasonable question to put, though it was never answered since he was not needed in Burma.

'He made me furious,' said my mother. 'Utterly wretched too. I had suffered so much. I couldn't believe what this foolish man was saying. I was not well and I had to rest. He made me cry into my pillow. Such cruelty! He stood there at the end of the bed, as if he were suggesting . . . well, no more than a visit to the weekend gymkhana. I wanted to throw something at him – a shoe or some-thing – but I was too upset and weak. I thought that we were going to be so happy. I thought, all through the war, if only I can get back to India. And now this. I didn't want him near me, not to touch me. Oh, I was so sick and so weak. All I wanted to do then was sleep, sleep. The doctor came but what use was he? What use are they ever?'

Soon after these events in Ambala, in about the third month of her pregnancy, my mother miscarried.

EIGHT

Interrupted Lessons

I N THE MORNING, in the wide bright dusty streets, sometimes we rode and sometimes we pushed our bicycles. It was
easy going – almost no traffic to worry us – and if we were early
we had time to practise the day's poem. This time, the words tripped
along nicely:

> On either side the river lie
> Long fields of barley and of rye,
> That clothe the wold and meet the sky.

It seemed a cheerful incantation, but in the present circumstance I
could make little sense of it. In this country, I saw a tangle of bushes,
thorn, tamarind, acacia, palm, with dust-devils and too much
distance in between. Somewhere over there, it was true, flowed a
big river. The town of Ferozepore had been founded on the old
high bank of the Sutlej, one of the five watery fingers of the Punjab.
But the reaches of that Himalayan run-off did not invite cosy
reflection. The spirit of the water was unreliable, a thing only
temporarily contained, moody amid snags and currents, shifting in a
blink from bland to ugly.

On the verandah of the school bungalow the teacher, a
Scotswoman in a long skirt and with two ropes of hair coiled in
Valkyrie-fashion about her ears, greeted us formally. Each day,
before lessons began, we had a group-recitation. We jumped up
eagerly and formed into a double line, vying with each other to
catch the teacher's eye, piping in high strident voices:

And by the moon the reaper weary,
Piling sheaves in uplands airy,
Listening, whispers ''Tis the fairy
   Lady of Shalott.'

We chanted this with enthusiasm while a dragon's breath of wind scoured the shores of the Sutlej.

The next poem to be learnt was 'The Daffodils'. It was, said our teacher rolling her 'r's, 'a grand wee poem for all of us in a foreign land.'

★

Had it not been for the similarity of the heat, and the bleached white light lying like hot drops of mercury on the eyelids, the municipality of Ferozepore – town and cantonment – promised to be easier on the body and the temper than Ambala. The town (Firozpur in the new orthography) owed its foundation and later development to two short but happy moments five hundred years apart. Firoz Shah had established it, in the middle of the fourteenth century. This Turkic ruler of the Delhi Sultanate had combined the indolence and savage unpredictability of oriental despotism with an artistic sense that yearned for the memorial of palaces and mosques and tombs, and for the more immediate gratification of gardens and arbours and fountains and the quiet plangency of the *sarod* and the stealthy tinkle of the dancing-girl's bells. For a few years, under the able administration of a Brahmin minister, the reign of Firoz cast a brief benevolence over the Punjab, and generations of peasants and townsmen saluted the memory of the old king (or, in reality, the memory of his minister Makbul).

The good times did not last. Makbul died and Firoz degenerated to a scandal of unhinged senility and impotent rage. Old days of misery returned and Ferozepore began to crumble and rot by the Sutlej, dwindling over centuries to a squalor of dogs and cow-dung amid a grandeur of ruins. From this state of near extinction it was rescued, in the mid-nineteenth century, by Sir Henry Lawrence, energetic soldier and loyal booster of British interests, who saw the advantage of the town's position and imprinted commercial enterprise, Victorian amplitude and bourgeois respectability on the old town-plan, adding broad tree-lined streets, substantial houses for business, a factory or two, and a wide circular promenade around the walls. This walk was lined with the villas and the gardens of men grown prosperous in the affairs of the East India Company. The military cantonment tacked on by the Raj after the shock of the Mutiny and the withering away of the Company did little to spoil this town that at least shook hands with the ideals of two very different civilizations.

But not a whisper of this long, embattled history reached us. I had to learn about it at a much later time. Miss McWhatshername instructed us in Faith, Duty and Deportment, with reading and writing and simple number-work, to which was added as an extra burnish the glory of 'Great Poems'. Sometimes, after lessons, we were shown the rudiments of Scottish country dancing.

Like all the British of the Raj, adult or child, I was a part of two worlds. I and my kind lived *on* India, not *in* it. One world − the superstructure of our lives provided by the Raj − was manifest, too plain to be missed by even the greatest dunderhead. The facts of this history supported us every moment of the day, in our houses waking and sleeping, in school, at work, in leisure and entertainment. We knew with an ingrained knowledge what the order of life should be and what was the limit of the permissible. At night, after the last drinks were cleared away, and the Indian bearer had dimmed the lights, emptied the ashtrays, plumped the cushions and given the silverware a final buff, he pulled the door closed softly, leaving us to rest in the cocoon of our contentment while he retreated into the limbo of the servants' quarters, in the shadowland of Indian India.

This other world, this shadowland, was a place for our averted eyes, almost secret − if not a dirty secret, at least a slightly disreputable tale, hardly mentioned in decent company. Of course, our elders knew that they could not escape the native world − it was the burden of most of their complaints. Struck by the same sun, we all trod the same parched earth under the wheeling kite's omniscient eye. The carrion crows lined up on the wall, giving their heads an ironic tilt as they took their usual opportunistic view, saw no more advantage in one of us than in another. The land, the climate, the day, the moments of existence belonged to all of us. But the two worlds moved, as it were, on parallel tracks, intimately close but separated by the indestructible veil of our histories. Our rules for living were not their rules.

This veil was less a problem for children than for adults. We could slip under it. Bicycling to school, gathering our little white tribe under the eye of our Rhinemaiden, struggling with her unlikely accent, wondering why the Scots Border country of Wallace and Bruce should be dear to our hearts too, counting the crowned heads of English monarchs on the wall-chart in the schoolroom (puzzling, Christ-like images, with soft brown beards, pale skin and doleful eyes), then embarking on yet another Lakeland journey from the *Lyrical Ballads*, we began each day strictly reined in by the expectations of our kind. And in the afternoons we swam in the clear blue pool of the Gymkhana Club, sipped lemonade, sat on the lawn in the lee of the big umbrellas while a regimental band of brown faces, immaculately smart, struck up the ritual tunes of our colonial music – popular pieces from Gilbert and Sullivan.

But released from the order of our conventional timetable we were free to improvise. Going home from the club we would follow the *bhishti*, laying the dust with the water from his goatskin as he edged slowly away from pseudo-Europe towards the ragged fringes of the cantonment bazaar. Greedily, we accepted nameless morsels from grubby stalls and keyhole shops where kids splashed water on the straw *tatty*, to make a cooling evaporation in the smouldering air. Ragamuffins kicked a ball of paper or cotton scraps into our path, challenging us to an impromptu game, jeering at our ineptitude (as yet we knew very little about team games).

'You want jiggy-jig?' they laughed at our innocence, pointing to shanties at the back of the bazaar. 'Very clean sister, she like jiggy-jiggy. You try?' Laughing, they swept on, hacking the rag-ball wildly over the *khud*-side. We blushed, not with shame but out of ignorance. We felt the presence of a mystery, but what it was we did not know.

*

One afternoon, in the leafy part of town inhabited by Europeans, I bent down to pat a dog. It was a handsome black labrador with a thick coat, lying restive but soulful in a patch of hot sunlight. As I ruffled the neck-fur and tugged at a drooping ear, the dog lurched up on its haunches and snapped at me, catching me on the cheekbone and breaking the skin.

As I staggered back I heard a lean major cry, 'Good grief, the boy's been bitten. Grab that hound.'

The dog, now completely quiet, was collared and led away, its tail curled between its hindlegs. Anxious faces peered at my cut, which was only superficial, and I was taken to the military dispensary. While an orderly was dabbing my face and cutting some sticking-plaster, I heard the word 'rabies' murmured.

To hear that word. It implied a world of horrors. Immediately, the dog and I were closely watched, as if we shared some guilt. Was the dog foaming from the mouth? Did I show signs of hydrophobia? Should the dog be killed and its brain sent for analysis? That would take time, the laboratory was far away. Should I begin the treatment anyway, the agonizing course of injections into the wall of the stomach? At night, I snivelled into my pillow, imagining a salivating jaw ripping into my flesh.

But the dog was normal, showing no signs of canine dementia. It had only been panting in the sun, suffering as we all did in the heat. My attention had made it jumpy and irritated. The fearful word 'rabies' ceased to be a crushing anxiety and retreated into some receptacle of warnings in the back of my brain. I began to see India in a new colour, a place with dangerous surprises hidden amid the privileges and the fun.

★

Sometimes Father took us to watch his Indian troops on some regimental occasion. In the declining day, when the worst of the heat had passed off, we sat on canvas chairs by the touchline of the sportsfield. A fine dust, pulverized by flying feet, blew off the bare surface. On a table by the halfway line, a big silver cup stood on a cloth with the regimental crest. An inter-company hockey match was under way and my father, trying not to look bored in the seat of honour reserved for the commanding officer, applauded carefully when others did the same. He hated sports. Hockey in particular was a penance to him, because when forced to play it he had been as maladroit as a lamed camel, and he was left-handed to boot.

But the Indian soldiers loved the game. They lashed into the ball with passion, protected only by puttees wound around the ankles. The ball skimmed the hard ground like a musket-shot, guided by the most delicate stick-work and sleight-of-hand, but pursued by violent oaths and furious gestures. I saw my father wince as a rush of Urdu hit his ears. The least of these expressions, I learnt later, were 'filthy pig' (to a Muslim) and 'your mother's a whore' (of more general application). But there was effervescence in their play, in the way they changed in a flash from apparent malevolence to joyful comradeship, from a brutal clash of sticks and whacks on the legs to radiant smiles and an arm across the shoulder. Sport, to us, seemed to mean earnest exercise, and modest sobriety in victory or defeat. To these sepoys it was fantasy, warfare, boasting, condescension, triumph, mercy. I began to perceive then, however unclearly, how these men might fight for real, with what raw fury in adversity, with what tears of compassion in relief. At the end of the game I saw the shy flush of approval on the faces of both winners and losers, the sigh for things done well as they lined up for the presentation of the cup. They were still grinning as they suffered my father's congratulations in halting Urdu.

We children had time on our hands, and an instinct to use it in low company. To help keep us out of mischief Father arranged for me and my brother to have riding lessons. A couple of times a week we went down to the lines of an Indian cavalry regiment (I forget which one). Out of the sun we passed into the high gloom of the stables, temporarily blinded by a deep wash of shadow, hearing the big animals shifting and blowing, their hoofs clunking hollowly on the wooden stalls. I smelt damp straw and urine, and the sweet odour from the brushed and curry-combed bodies.

Beyond the stables, by the side of the schooling ring, the risaldar-major awaited us. This native soldier, the senior Indian NCO in the regiment, was traditionally a figure of lofty importance, even grandeur. The essential intermediary between British officers and native troops, he was the pivot on which the well-being of the regiment rested. If the balance was wrong then the life of the regiment was likely to be cockeyed and tipped over into resentments. And good risaldar-majors knew their place and worth. Usually, they measured up to their own estimation – ramrod figures with handsome cavalry moustaches and the stamp of command on weathered faces. The shine on their riding boots had the moonlit sheen of a deep still lake; the cummerbund about the long tunic was placed to an inch; the ends of the tight-wound turban, with the regimental colours aslant, waved bravely below the high peak of the *pugree*.

The risaldar-major came forward a little stiffly on legs getting old and too used to riding. His salute to my father had the dignity of respect without a hint of subservience. Formally, he turned to us children and saluted again, this time with a smile. 'Ah, young sahibs,' he said, 'come. Now, we ride.'

I did not like it. I was frightened. The beast was too large, the glossy brown back a continent too wide for my puny legs to encompass. Unable to get a grip I felt the bruising bump of the hard cavalry saddle. The risaldar-major stood by the ring with a long whip in his hand. With the tip of the whip he stirred the horse, giving it more a caress or a tickle than a stroke. 'Huh,' he whispered, 'huh,' or for more urgency a rapid 'hah, hah, hah,' using an equine language that the horse understood perfectly. Arching its neck it moved into a deliberate rocking-horse trot, round and round the ring, for me an interminable torture. I held the reins, but for all the control I had I might just as well have been on a fairground merry-go-round.

'Good, good,' cried my instructor who was also my tormentor, 'back more straight, please. Bottom up down. *Up* and down, *up* and down. You see, very nice, very nice riding.'

After an unpleasant expanse of time I was allowed off. I never did get used to it. On every occasion I fell trembling from the high horse-back into tough Indian hands.

Afterwards, the ground once more stable under foot, our instructor used to take us to his quarters for light refreshment. Gravely, the risaldar-major ushered us under a low lintel into a small compound surrounded by a mud wall. His wife was waiting to greet us, smiling and salaaming. She was in Punjabi dress, a long tunic and light silky pantaloons nipped in at the ankles. Her hair, raven-black with a few streaks of grey, was loosely gathered at the nape of her neck, and she had a little gold stud in the side of her nose. As she moved her hands, bangles tinkled. She spoke not a word of English, but the lean of the shoulders and the spread of the arms expressed welcome and conviviality. We all settled on the cloth placed on the ground, my brother and I awkwardly, the risaldar-major and his wife with graceful ease. Between us were plates with small eats and titbits, and thick glass tumblers. We nibbled flaky pastries and small soggy balls so sweet that they made the teeth ache. We were offered weak tea without milk, or fresh fruit juice.

There was much gesturing towards food but not much was said, we being almost silent out of nerves and embarrassment, the soldier out of dignity, and his wife for lack of English. I looked at her covertly, as much as I dared without open rudeness. In the midst of a winning smile was a mouthful of bad teeth. But taking note of her from her neat toes to her thick luxuriant hair, sensing the warmth from the tawny brown skin, losing myself with blushes in the impenetrable deep of her dark eyes, hearing the small music of her bangles and the slithery rustle of her clothes, I thought I had never come across anything so beautiful.

★

The dog took up most of the space on the narrow seat. It was a muscular bull-terrier, brindle in colour, with the eerie pinkish eyes of the breed and an affection for humans. It liked to nuzzle up close, even to strangers, shoving a powerful shoulder into the back of the nearest leg, and any unoccupied lap soon found itself a pillow for a blunt head with a look of loopy devotion. At this moment, the head was in my lap and the compact body was lolling at ease along the seat, cramping me into a corner, against the shudders of the window. A thin dribble from between a set of wicked teeth was making a damp sticky patch on my shorts.

The dog, which belonged to one of my father's fellow officers in Ferozepore, had been pining in the heat of the plains. For this reason it was seconded into our family and was travelling with my mother, my brother and myself on the narrow-gauge railway between Kalka and Simla. We were all promised the relief of the hill station, the luxury of a Himalayan view together with warm days and cool nights at 7000 feet.

A visit to Simla was almost as good as a passage home. For the members of the Raj it was a refuge, a settled place for the heart amid the ravages and indignities of their responsibility in this perplexing conquered land. Simla was entirely a British invention. In 1819 the Political Agent for the Hill States took a virgin tract of mountain and put up the first dwelling, no more than a little thatched cottage. His successor, a certain Lieutenant Kennedy, built the first permanent house. Ten years later there were still only thirty houses. But by the end of the century Simla was a sizeable town of great importance, the Headquarters of the Commander-in-Chief, the summer seat of the Governor-General, and the summer capital of the Government of India. There, if anywhere in India, the members of the Raj could feel physically and spiritually safe.

At that altitude it was a pleasure to breathe the air. But first we had to struggle through the throng to the air. My mother, as usual, was making a meal of the complications – the dog, her children, the luggage, our destination. She was both stern and flustered, going from frown to dither in a moment. My brother had charge of the dog, straining at its lead, its claws skittering on the floor. In the native maul that enveloped the arrival of the train, even the most hardened hustler or beggar backed away from the panting bull-terrier, with its fierce rictus of a grin, its head like an inquisitive python, and its over-friendly tail whipping bare legs. Not until we were outside, with the rickshaws arranged, did my mother relax the stiff set of her head and try a few sniffs of the mountain air. A piece of her burden, some of the eternal ambiguity of India, slipped away. Even the over-excited dog, sprinkling spittle over our shoes, received a consoling pat.

I know now that she was trying to put behind her the recent shocks of her marriage, the loss of her baby, and my father's too enthusiastic militarism. Where better to re-compose herself than in Simla? She could begin immediately. How pleasant it was to bowl along streets that had some clear, assignable purpose, leading to shops and hotels and banks and government offices. Too much of

Indian life had been a muddle to her, indescribable routes that
merged into a labyrinthine maze without exits. A little mysterious
exoticism did not go amiss in the East (but like spices in the native
curries it could be over-done for the English palate), but at bottom
she wanted clearer signposts stamped with messages from her race
and place and society.

Now, here we were in the Mall, heading in the direction of
Viceregal Lodge, going to an hotel that lay under Observatory Hill.
What could be more reassuring than that? Behind, to the east, the
tall green peak of Jakko rose up at the end of the spur, sweet-
smelling with a pervasive scent of deodar cedars and pine resin.
Westward from Jakko, the town rambled half a dozen lazy miles
along the ridge to the bald lump of Prospect Hill. Slipping down
from the ridge, on the southern slope towards the plains,
bungalows, buildings and low government blocks peeped from the
trees, lying like contented beasts in the greenery. Rhododendron
and hydrangea cascaded out of the woods, waiting to threaten the
paths with a seasonal flood of blossom.

If you half-closed your eyes, and dreamed a little, discounting the
bazaar and the evidence of humanity on the streets, you could
imagine yourself in some pleasant Alpine town temporarily
occupied by a transient oriental circus.

*

We had other business in Simla. My brother and I were to be put
to school, to receive a proper, British education, the sort that the
little cantonment school in Ferozepore could not provide. We
would go to Bishop Cotton School, an institution for European
boys founded in 1866 in thanksgiving for the deliverance of the
British from the horrors of the Mutiny in 1857. It was accepted that
this school taught the real virtues appropriate to imperial
responsibility.

For some reason we did not go there at once. We had an initial
period, perhaps a time of trial or cramming for a level that might be
beyond us, of private tuition with Miss Smythe. She seemed rather
ancient to me, a relic of a departed gentility. But despite her age this
kindly lady was almost too lively for her maiden dignity, in tweed
skirts and cashmere knitwear, with an optimistic cast on life.

Her view of what constituted adequate knowledge in the young was rather quirky.

'Now, boys,' she said, sizing us up on the first visit, 'what do you know about Harry Lauder?'

I knew nothing about the Scottish comedian, but it hardly mattered because she was already hurrying on, gesturing with a thin vivacious hand around the Victorian gloom of her little parlour. From then on she usually had a surprise question, a little time-bomb left to tick in the wastes of our ignorance. Did we prefer rickshaws to tongas? Had we heard of trade unions? Where and what was the Taj Mahal? What was the maiden name of King George's queen? Did we know what a *juggernaut* was? What countries did we pass on our journey from England to Bombay? What was seven times nine, and nine times twelve? Would we like some *kulfi*? Should she show us her collection of small porcelain dolls?

These and another thousand sprightly hares sprang up in her lively mind, flushed out by an invincible curiosity, and once she had raised an attractive quarry she chased it up hill and down dale, hardly caring where her investigations might lead. It was an approach to learning that enchanted me. I began to see the world as a vast kaleidoscope of iridescent facts that could be fitted into any number of patterns. With a mere turn of the head and a rearrangement of the eye the pattern changed. It was the cast of mind that was important.

It amazed me that she made no invidious distinction between British and Indian. The intertwined histories shifted unpredictably between heroes and villains, who were not quite those you would expect. Her imagination was at ease in both England and India, and she did not hesitate to draw lessons for British children from the daily life of the Indian streets. I stood in her window, my head in a whirl, trying to apply her principle of inclusiveness. From that window I looked on a large natural bowl into which was stirred pell-mell the mixture of our lives. Cars and donkeys, turbans and topees, a large church and a small *gurdwara*, scuffed earth and tarmac, banks and go-downs, a cold-water standpipe by a runnel of raw sewage, imperial soldiers and Nepalese porters, pretty dogs on leads and pariah dogs with sores. But looking at the faces in the street, white and brown and every shade in between, I could not perceive from the buzz and the activity the essential colour of the soul.

We did not stay long with Miss Smythe. I missed her, though I left more dizzy than enlightened, somewhere between sunlight and fog.

★

I had been ill with bronchitis. The cool and the damp of the hills had some disadvantages. I was confined to bed and shared my seclusion with the bull-terrier who volunteered to divide the bed with me. Growling playfully it contested my pillows and sheets, and when my mother came to read me a daily helping of Kipling (Simla and the world of Mrs Hauksbee were becoming real to me) she had to squeeze herself on the edge of the bed between sprawling paws. I grew fond of that dog.

So we were friends, the dog and I, and when the time came, after I was recovered, to take the dog for a good walk I pleaded with my brother – who was in charge – to let the dog off the lead. A fit young dog on a lead is a sorry beast. The day was warm, calm, without a sign of trouble, with few people about, so my brother agreed. We strolled with the dog at our heels – it was well-trained, up to a point – until we approached a crossroads where a smart Indian man in European clothes stood talking to a companion. Sitting at their feet was a small spaniel. As we came up the spaniel became excited, yapping and jumping, starting towards the bull-terrier but still wagging its tail. It was only a puppy and no doubt had something inquisitive and civil in mind.

But the bull-terrier, for all its fawning on humans, could not abide other dogs. If it thought itself challenged, it went for the other dog at once. The short hair between the shoulder-blades bristled, the ears went back, the brutal muzzle slit into a snarl. A low rumble reverberated in the deep chest, the thick muscles bunched. Without any preliminary, no testing or probing, it launched itself straight at the throat of the spaniel. The jaws closed and locked, the bulging legs braced, the fearful head twisted and turned, shaking the poor spaniel like a cornered rat. There was an appalling, dangerous contentment in the growl. The bull-terrier was set for the kill.

The smart-looking Indian bawled at us to control our dog. But horrified though we were, my brother and I were helpless. No orders could penetrate that concentrated lust to kill. Then the owner of the spaniel took the chain for his own dog, which was lying uselessly over his arm, doubled it into a short length and taking both hands began to whip the bull-terrier with all his strength. The links of the chain bit into the brindled coat but to no purpose. The deadly jaws clamped the windpipe of the little dog until the life was crushed out of it and the limp body trailed like a half-discarded coat. Then the bull-terrier was satisfied. It let go and lay quietly panting, registering no ill-effect from the blows of the chain. But we, the human spectators, stared at each other without comprehension, our blankness being an apology for our helplessness. After a moment or two I burst into sudden, racking sobs.

Two days later, in a soft and darkening evening, an Indian lady in a sari came into the courtyard of our hotel and called repeatedly for my mother in a voice rising hysterically. My mother came out onto the first-floor gallery that ran around the courtyard and stood clutching the rail, looking down at the lady below. My mother's knuckles were white and she would go no further. 'Yes, what do you want?' she asked tentatively, though she surely knew the answer. Then into the lengthening shadows the elegant lady spewed a torrent of invective in which reasoned complaint in English for the murder of her dog was flooded out from time to time with spurts in Hindi and a confusion of barrack-room swear words. My mother was transfixed. The complaint she could understand. She had sympathy for the lady in the sari and would give her compensation. But the degree of passion seemed crazy, excessive. It betrayed her breeding. No dog was worth such a ridiculous show. My mother had no words to reply. The naked grief and hatred left her rooted with both embarrassment and fear. Her face was ghostly pale. Hardly ever had I seen her so bereft. After a while she turned her back and went to her room, gently closing her door on cries still wailing into a darkening world.

★

Then our schooling began at Bishop Cotton, and we were not

spared the full British treatment. Deprivation, sparse rations, knees raw from compulsory games, the cold sneer of authority, learning driven by the ruler or cane. In shirts and shorts of tough cotton we submitted to a discipline dutifully preserved for us by generations of God-fearing mercantilists and soldiers. It was education by duress in the old hearty manner, fruition through blood and tears. Meekly, we accepted it and even gave thanks in chapel for the privilege of our pain. Our teachers promised us that it instilled what they called 'backbone'.

This method, laying each boy under the burden of an oppressive group-psychology, tended to make us vulgar and coarse. Under instruction we were sullen, sly, ganging together for solidarity. 'Please, sir, it was Mullins. We saw him. Jimmy gave him a whack and then Mullins threw the ball at him. It missed and broke the window.' Collectively we hid behind circumstantial sneaking, giving time and place. Imbued with this herd instinct we found it easier to learn by rote. Every morning a sour-faced bachelor with a persistent cough took our junior class through the multiplication tables. We stood in a small bare room ringing with voices, and the chanted repetition had something like the effect of a mantra. Eyes almost closed we swayed slightly to the simple arithmetic. In a similar manner I could catalogue, in a sing-song voice and without mistakes, all the dates of the reigns of the kings of England. Now, I still remember most of that farrago (with some lapses), such is the force of heavy-handed imprint on a young mind. But what did I know of Chandragupta or Ashoka, of Akbar or Aurangzeb? Those names and their deeds were a blank to me. And Hindu, Muslim, Buddhist, Jain, Sikh were labels without content, no more. Our God inhabited an austere Anglican chapel, though my brother and I, as Catholics, were conscientiously sent by car each Sunday to the RC Cathedral. That far was enough. Beyond that, the school washed its hands of us. To go whoring after the Scarlet Woman of Rome was a personal matter, a lapse in moral taste not very far from the worship of Shiva or Vishnu or Buddha. A superstition, a blot.

Even for the meekest of us, the straitjacket of our schooling chafed unbearably after a time. We had a sense that we were unnecessary prisoners bound by rules irrelevant to the continent we inhabited. In the daily life of children we knew more of India than our parents suspected. So in the breaks, and outside the set hours of lessons, we burst fizzing into the playground, drawn towards the scrublands and borders of native territory. We were bubbling like soda-bottles, and as likely to overflow. Sick of puritans with canes we wanted the loose, messy entanglement of India. We raided neighbouring fields and brought back poles for makeshift goalposts. We traded the blackest words we knew, in both English and Hindustani, with local lads who despised us for our feeble resistance to the iron bonds of our regimentation. In superior numbers we drove them off with stones and clods of dirt. Then peace was made and hands shaken with droll formality, and trade began in comics and sweets and *pan* and *bidis*. Occasionally, playfulness would erupt into a rough-house, and when we caught a laggard we kicked him thoroughly. Then tired of football or trading or fighting we retreated to the safety of school grounds and hurled ourselves into a favourite game. We divided into small groups, under the banner of either 'Maratha' or 'Moghul', and marked out our positions. The aim of this contest was to attack, gain and hold territory. It was a game that required much barging and wrestling, sudden jumps, swift movement, deceptive feints, strategic retreats. It needed both strength and cunning, big louts but also some smart brains.

Years later, when Marathas and Moghuls ceased to be just names to me, I looked back on these games as an unwitting initiation into the very Indian world of the *Arthashastra*. Kautilya's ancient military treatise taught that subterfuge, treachery and guile, together with sudden and rapid movement, were the best principles of military strategy. I thought then of Sivaji, the founder of Maratha power, who in 1659, during a truce, welcomed the Moghul general Afzal Khan with an embrace, and in doing so stabbed him in the back with the blades of the *bagh-nakh*, the steel 'tiger's claw'.

★

I was ill again. Showing off on the rim of a steep gully I fell and dislodged a rock that tumbled onto my ankle and cracked a bone. The onset of complications forced me into hospital for a short time. It was a free and easy place, with laxity bordering on negligence. Like some marauding pirate, with my leg in full-length plaster, I hobbled into any ward that took my fancy, whatever the risk of infection. The Indian who looked after my room – I never knew if he was nurse, orderly or cleaner – showed me how to make a hairy rabbit out of a mango stone that had been sucked clean.

I left hospital with a family of these little rabbits and with a few scattered pockmarks; for though no one told me then, in hospital I had been exposed to, and recovered from, a mild attack of smallpox.

In India, as Sivaji knew and incautious Afzal Khan did not, it was wise to keep a careful look over your shoulder.

NINE

Victory

AFTER ONE TERM at Bishop Cotton we left Simla. But we were travelling too much. Journeys that had seemed in the beginning to be unusual fun were becoming wearisome. I wanted to settle down, but now we were on our way to Delhi. Where were we going in the huge and sprawling city? Leaving the railway station not even the tonga-wallah was quite sure of our destination, driving twice around Connaught Circus before he decided on the right exit road.

Delhi had a different air, more febrile and thunder-brewed than elsewhere; even a child could sense the change of mood. In the morning, I liked to watch my father shave. The bearer brought a tray with a cup of tea and a mug of very hot water. Sipping tea slowly my father discarded his dressing-gown, revealing the high wings of his thin shoulder-blades poking from a sleeveless vest. Soberly he carried the hot water into the raw cement hutch that served as our bathroom. Grubby morning light floated down from a high aperture that was more grille than window, flecking blotches of shadow over the ochre water-stains in the basin. As he made his methodical and unvarying preparation I watched from the doorway, chewing a finger. I liked to see the white snowdrift of the soapsuds vigorously swirled onto the face, and then the clean path cut by the safety razor as my father cleared a line of soap from his temple to his jaw. He kept his head up and made the skin tight by pinching with his forefinger and thumb the loosening drift of flesh over his adam's apple. Then he steered carefully around the bristly bank of his moustache. There was something timeless and hieratic in his daily ritual. As he made his appearance trim, so he set his mind in order for the coming day.

He wiped the excess suds from his face with a small hand-towel and straightened his long back, thrusting his dark, neatly combed head among the motes swaying in the weak rays of window-light. I thought he looked drawn – tired or despondent. I could not quite express it, but why so much weight and solemnity in such a simple ritual?

The city was full of rumours that we could not fail to catch. The name Subhas Chandra Bose hung in the air, meaning nothing to children, but causing long looks of consternation in adults. At morning coffee among the army wives, and with the early-evening tots of whisky, Bose's name would suddenly spurt and flare, a dangerous ignition threatening some explosion. Bose himself was dead, killed very recently in a plane crash on the way to Japan. But three men (I learnt later that they were a Hindu, a Muslim and a Sikh, all officers in Bose's revolutionary Indian National Army) were awaiting trial in the Red Fort, a few miles to our north in the Old City. *Jai Hind* – 'Long live India' – the rallying-cry of the INA, still produced a roaring in British ears. There had been mutinies in the RAF, ornery young flyers determined to get home to England as soon as possible, followed by mutiny in the Indian Air Force. Even now anger and impatience were fretting away the discipline on the Bombay ships of the Indian Navy. Bold graffiti appeared on the walls of the shore station HMIS *Talwar.* 'Revolt Now' and 'Kill the British White Bastards'.

'The natives are getting bolshie,' a memsahib said, waving her cigarette under the nose of an Indian servant squirting soda into her whisky. 'Oh, definitely. We'll have to do something, you know, there comes a time when kindness just won't wash. I hear that even the Auk is worried. He had to slap down one of those cheeky Congress *babus* the other day.'

And my father confirmed later that the Auk – the Commander-in-Chief Sir Claude Auchinleck – was indeed worried. That loyal, rugged, devoted soldier of the Raj, with forty years of Indian service and paternal towards all Indians, whom he admired and would have said that he loved could he have got the words out of his choked heart, was only an incomplete politician and the course of Indian history was raging beyond him.

My father was suffering too. He also loved India, and had not enough words to express it. He had been summoned to Delhi, to work in the military secretariat that was planning the whole future of the Indian Army. No one but a fool doubted that independence was coming, and coming soon. India in wartime had earned that, at least. The post-war election of a Labour government in England had waved the express from the siding of history, and Congress and the Muslim League in India had stoked the fire-box with madcap enthusiasm, despite the unresolved problems of the religious and ethnic divide. Gandhi, impish and unreadable, with weak hams and watery eyes, drove from one side of the foot-plate, Jinnah, a thin pillar of rectitude, from the other. The train was unstoppable. My father welcomed its arrival. He had always voted Labour (a rather astonishing thing in an Indian Army officer). He believed in self-determination, and he wanted justice done to India. He set to work, not unwillingly but conscious of inner pain, to dismantle the basis of his life.

★

The tonga put us down at the King Edward VII Hostel, a spare uncomfortable block with sharp edges somewhere in Lutyens-land, between Old Delhi to the north and an older Delhi in the south.

We were adrift in vast urban reaches, tumbled topography lying layer upon layer, formed and reformed by storms of history, but we were without a compass. Rock and river, red sandstone stiffening into marble, Hindu opulence metamorphosing into chaste Muslim, little temples buckling and sinking under the load of much bigger shrines or forts or palaces, and out of this urban humus odd and graceful features arising, pillars, columns, towers, minarets, giant walls, bulb-domes, tombs, heavy mosques as large as city blocks, the light tracery of a devotional building as small as a doll's house. And ruins crumbling into further ruins, piecemeal structures with functions assigned and re-assigned according to conquests and masters and religions, then neglected, then forgotten, then re-invented, then abandoned, part of the detritus of the human hive, the workers ever busy, using, improvising, jettisoning, respectful to the past in some general way but not remembering just what was *that* bit of the past.

And between the ideal-city of Shah Jehan in the north and the ideal-city of the Lodi kings and of Firoz Shah in the south stood New Delhi, the lump of Anglo-India dreamed and engineered by Lutyens and his sidekick Baker to supersede the past, to out-shout the dynasties – Hindu or Muslim – and put the cap of worthy splendour on the colourful but disorderly raiment of a thousand years gone.

We were placed among these heavy swells and sea-changes but I hardly saw them, the evidence of time being for the most part below the horizon of a boy's interest. My father was taken up with the business of empire, working long hours on plans that knocked him breathless, with his career abruptly against the wall. My mother, left alone in our ground-floor quarters, doors wide onto rank grass and the hopeless complication of the Delhi skyline, did not go out if she could help it. She had no curiosity about history or its local tangles, no architectural sense, no interest in antiquities, no particular feeling for Hindu or Muslim culture. Even less thought for Sikh or Jain or Buddhist or Parsi. She was fond of small pretty things – material and jewellery and carving and glassware and rugs and Benares brass – and would admire them if brought to them, and even buy a specimen if it were offered for a slight sum. But she would not willingly stir for anthropology, history or art, and preferred the minimum of movement even for shopping. The climate, of course, was rough on fair-skinned Northerners with freckles, if they were reckless with sunlight.

After breakfast, the bearer came for household orders, standing with a kind of alert humility while my mother made her list. With a wave of the hand she conjured up some simple tasks and dismissed him with a brief nod, hardly noticing his departure, cracked brown heels padding below the stiff whites of his servant's clothes. Then she was free, but for what? Food or meals were no bother to her, since we ate in the hostel dining-room. She retreated to the intimate world of army wives, a sorority held together, as far as I could see, by cigarette smoke and loud laughter and the minute investigation of petty scandals. These gatherings were leisurely affairs, well-coiffured heads thrown back in the long chairs, feet at rest on a pouffe, a cheerful tinkle of ice. From the outside it was hard to see where the fun lay. Children were not welcome – in fact definitely an encumbrance. 'Off you go now,' my mother would say impatiently, when we weren't at school, 'I can't have you squabbling and making a rowdy mess in here. You can see I'm busy.' Could I see that? In the mornings, it seemed to me, she was taken up with events I did not understand. In the afternoons she slept a little.

So we went out, eagerly and with a superabundance of energy given to the young by the blessing of sun and heat. For us, life in India was lived out of doors. Freedom for the body, released from the tightness of four walls and hardly restrained by the weather, allows a certain freedom in the mind. There was so much strange stuff to note – humans laying out the accumulated wares of their consciousness. My view, I think now, came to be all the wider for my life in the open, more embracing, more pregnant with evidence for a future understanding; for of course the order of history was not clear to me at that time. Nor did I look systematically or dutifully. The vision of the young is not adjusted for sightseeing or the guidebook. But as Delhi was brimful with so many adventures left by megalomania or artistic genius, I could not avoid the brilliant onrush of powerful images.

The hopeless jumble of these stored images: the wild vital human pulses of street-life on Chandni Chowk surging through the Lahore Gate into Lal Qila – the Red Fort – and there transformed into the great running rhythms of Moghul architecture, pure energy transmuted into the purity of noble order; the vast emptiness of the courtyard of the Jama Masjid – the Friday Mosque – lording it over the suffocating sprawl of the Kinari and Chawri bazaars, and the nostril-clenching stench of the Fish Market, offering the peace of prayer for the hagglers and bruisers of commerce; the partial greeds and desires, the race for the winning-post, reconciled on the knees with head touching the earth before the Oneness of Allah; the long urban journey south from Old Delhi, the modern road effacing time, making a blankness of the past out of which arise only the melancholy of tombs, of Lodi kings and Moghul emperors, meandering back to the tall graceful minaret of the Qutb Minar from where the historical cry of the *muezzin* celebrated victory over the

Tomari Rajputs and the first enduring triumph of Islam in India, the conqueror Qutb-ud-din raising his memorial buildings on the remains of many Jain and Hindu temples with the help of Hindu craftsmen and the use of Hindu motifs. The present recapitulating the past.

And then after 800 years, with the revenge of time, Independence Day, through the intervention of the British, gave the city back to the Hindus. The British Raj, too, left its mark, which a child of the Raj, residing in the Edward VII Hostel only a few hundred yards from the King's Way, could not help but notice.

I see now in my mind the long triumphal route from the Viceroy's mansion on Raisina Hill to India Gate. The sweeping away of historical clutter in favour of a new imperial vision. I see now the monumental masonry, rhetorical, overblown but powerfully evocative, lonely amid wind-drifts of tarmac bordered by the slight scum on the waters of the ornamental ponds. In my imagination I feel the heaviness, the gravity, of it all, but I see no *people*. It was a gift to vacant space, that should have been populated but was not, by a new imperial order in India.

★

It was a surprise to a British boy to discover that we were not the only foreigners in Delhi. In fact, were we foreigners? We had within us a presumption of ownership. But suddenly the Americans had arrived. One day – I cannot recall how or why we met – a rangy specimen of irrepressible manhood came into the lives of my brother and myself: Sergeant Brad of the US Army. He was a tall gingery enthusiast for life, with a crew-cut and deep scars of acne on his neck, broken veins in his cheeks, and a nose that had peeked over the rim of many a glass. He seemed to have a kitbag full of bonhomie. He accepted us as he would a couple of tail-wagging dogs, both amused and puzzled by our blank ignorance of the American way. He himself, from some dreary sweep of Midwestern cornfields, had never been east of the Missouri until 1943, but he regarded the known facts of American life as the equivalent of universal knowledge.

'Howd'you like that!' he would roar with noisy wonder. 'Y'mean you didn't *know* that?'

He liked to take us in hand and get us alongside reality. He was proud to be American and eager to lay out the benefits for a more general view. To our joy, he was prodigal with Wrigley's gum and Coca-Cola and American comics, and for these at least we were willing to suffer instruction. He took us thoroughly into US Army life.

'You guys hungry?' he would enquire, hustling us into the mess hall. 'OK, soldier, move your butt over and let these little fellas get in here. Hey, Lenny, how about some chow for our Limey friends?'

Then I had set before me dishes that seemed incongruous in the extreme. Many of them had a vile look about them: toast fried in egg with syrup poured over it; sweet pancakes with bacon, again with syrup; chicken ringed with pineapple; pies made out of pumpkin. Often I hesitated and this slowness seemed part of the unsatisfactory way I ate.

'Lemme show you,' said kindly Brad. 'Cut 'em up with your knife and then lay it aside. Switch the fork to that hand and kinda spear the pieces one by one, so you don't get in a mess.'

It looked to me like a laborious and unnecessary process. But I was willing to try, waiting for the inevitable question, 'Ready for another Coke?'

I was.

Soon, we ran into trouble at home on account of our American friend. The comics did it – that particular type of American comic – those depraved pictures of cruelty and pain, high-coloured, with males mightily muscled and crotch-bulging, and females pared to large curves and a dab of tiny panties. Used to the *Beano* and the *Dandy* I was aghast at such a graphic celebration of violence and sadism. Yet the combination of naturalism in portraiture and twisted fantasy in the storyline had a strong subversive hold. Evil looked muscular, daring and zestful. The depravity was heroic.

We hid the comics under the mattress or at the back of the high shelf in the clothes cupboard, but that was not enough to escape my mother's keen eye and ever-exploring hand. She took a comic to my father, being unable to look at such muck herself. Father was severe. Where had this come from? Oh, we said airily, those comics were everywhere on the US base, which was true and didn't incriminate

Sergeant Brad. Then father spoke to us of common decency and the horrors of violence. He made no comment on the latent sexuality of the sadism, on the priapic thrust of the drawing. But he ordered us to cut out all comics from the base, and in general to keep away from American GIs as much as possible. There were elements in their culture it was best not to see. They lived life to another plan, which was energetic and open (my father did not object to that), but sowed seeds for too much grief and violence.

Still we sneaked away to the base and occasionally Sergeant Brad drove us home. One early afternoon, being rather late, we pressed for a lift and he jumped to it with his usual good humour. He drove with exhilarating carelessness, a boot resting on the cut-away door-frame of the Jeep, his face beaming out like a lighthouse. He was slightly drunk, though I didn't see it then, taking his erratic runs and swerves as natural American elan. He insisted on coming right to our quarters. My mother, who was home alone, greeted him with a cautious and reserved handshake. Good manners demanded polite-ness, but he was only a sergeant and an American at that, and he was acting distinctly odd. Too jolly and friendly, respectful but with an under-current of almost winking intimacy. My mother, when she was socially nervous, put on a distant haughtiness and disdain. She offered him a glass of beer, which was certainly a mistake, and indicated a chair into which he dropped heavily with a profusion – too many – of thanks. It looked as if adults were going to start chatting, so we boys quickly got out of there.

Years later my mother told me what had happened, the embarrassment of it still making her eyebrows shoot up in surprise.

'I had such trouble with your Sergeant Brad,' she said accusingly. 'He began talking such enthusiastic rubbish. Very disconnected, you know. And then he insisted on showing me photos of all his family, though he could barely get his wallet out of his back pocket. Such coarse faces, all grinning and sunburnt, and the little girls in such unsuitable dresses. Everyone seemed to live in a jumble – people, dogs, cars, farm implements, and long ugly fields in the background. He'd had one or two beers by this time, and then the photos started to make him maudlin. He kept appealing to me as a mother – I had no idea what he meant – and then he squeezed a few tears from his eyes and insisted that he'd like to come and sit next to me. Well, that just simply wasn't on, was it? He got up and lurched rather, in my direction. I was horrified, so I rushed to the door and called for the bearer. That was enough to sober him up a bit, and the bearer and I were able to get him out of the house, though he was unsteady and ready to make a grab for me, if only to keep himself straight. He kept saying "Ma'am this, and Ma'am that" and how he hoped there was no offence, and what "great little boys" I had. And then he almost fell on his nose getting into his jeep. Really, it was dangerous to let him drive, but I couldn't wait to get shut of him. And do you know, when I went back into the sitting-room, I found that he'd leaked a puddle onto the cushion of the chair!'

Poor Sergeant Brad, so excitable, so lonely, so confiding. He was very far from home. The war-world had given him harder matter than he had learnt how to chew. He wanted reassurance – the mother's hand. There was some sexual expectation there too, with his itch for love unsalved by the mysteries of Eastern coupling. But he wanted to be soothed as much as he wanted to be excited. He wanted the security of family, and in some sense he had tried to burrow into ours. But at this, my mother *did* take offence.

After this, Sergeant Brad dropped away. We lost an American friend, and our best source for Coca-Cola. But by chance, I had one more encounter with the US Army. Some time later, after a children's party, I was offered a lift home in a US staff-car. Instead of a utilitarian jeep, this was an enormous Packard, and my fellow passenger – in the grey quilted upholstery of the back seat was a US Army general. I did not catch the name of my benefactor as we rustled through streets suddenly drained of noise by the tight-fitting windows. He was a dapper man, extremely bright and sharp with sharp creases, and a fore-and-aft cap cleaving the air like the bow of an Atlantic liner. He had an affable manner, not at all put out to be chatting with a young boy, and he told me many interesting and gory details from the Japanese campaigns in which he had served. Among the enemy he had formed a passion – so he told me – for the art, the mystique, of samurai swords. He admired everything about them – the glamour, the workmanship, the beauty, the efficiency, the murderous ease of the swift cutting strokes. He collected them avidly, and just that day another specimen had come into his hands. He had it in the car. Then reaching behind he took a sword from the back window-ledge and began to slide the slippery silver serpent out of its black lacquered sheath. I stared at the blade, with a chased design – a dragon? – that undulated towards the still hidden point.

'Just look at that,' said the general with rapt attention. 'I've seen one of these beauties slice right through the stock of a rifle.'

With a sigh he snapped the blade back into the sheath, giving the lacquer a quick rub with his sleeve. 'My goodness, yes,' he murmured, 'that's some piece of work.' Somehow I got the impression that whatever had happened in the Far East was fully justified if it put such treasures into the hands of the connoisseurs.

★

Amid the acts of war, any strange city that keeps itself at peace though still big and bustling, will be a refuge, however alien the place and language. Delhi had its share of poor souls sprung loose from familiar moorings, floundering on a tide they could not fathom. They got a grip on any plank that came by and struck against the current, to break out of the rush towards oblivion. Pride and some dignity were the first things lost in shipwreck. If you were wise, you let them go without tears. Desperation, a schoolmaster told me once, gives greater strength than a pedigree back to Charlemagne.

Two of those souls bobbed up on our little portion of the beach. A Czech husband and wife came knocking on the doors of the Edward VII Hostel carrying a large black portfolio. They were vague gentle beings, bordering on defeated late middle-age, with little to set against the flood but the husband's slight talent as an artist. He did portraits, in pencil, ink or pastel, specializing in children. Laying out the specimens from the portfolio they haggled quietly in cracked English, relying on helplessness more than on argument. The prices were not high. Most of the discussion centred on how many sittings would be needed. He would rather not be rushed – he had old-world standards of commitment. It was the task of the wife to keep young sitters quiet by reading them stories.

My mother was drawn towards this couple, feeling their isolation in a tough world and admiring their dogged determination to make the best of their resources. The portraits, though pleasantly done and lifelike, were hardly more than competent. But the Czechs themselves were pathetic in the proper sense, being the cause of heightened emotion in others. So an agreement was struck and a number of sittings booked, to take place in our quarters. The problem then was to get my brother and myself lassooed and in place and settled for a half-hour or so of boredom. No one had asked if *we* wanted our portraits done.

At that time we were seriously employed learning how to smoke. Both our parents were veritable chimneys. The cost, for army officers, was negligible. Cigarettes piled up in our home like log-booms in flood-tide. The tins of fifty Players, the foil ripped off, were never far from any needy hand. To slip a few in the pocket was the work of a moment. It hardly seemed like stealing. Then we retired to a broken wilderness at the end of the grounds where a great many cement bags had been dumped, hardening through monsoon rains into a fortress of many runs and tunnels in which secretive boys could conduct certain experiments. Puffing away with anguished faces, trying to inhale, we were testing which was more satisfactory, our parents' Players or the native bidis of the bazaar, a mixture (or so I was told) of cow-dung and tobacco wrapped very thinly in a coarse leaf.

So sometimes I was rather groggy when summoned to a sitting. When we were settled in the right light – the artist worked on us both at the same time, in small attacks – the wife began to read from a well-thumbed volume of English folk-tales that she dug out of a deep disorderly bag. Her voice was clogged with strange stresses and pronunciation. When she tried to put some animation into the story, accents clung to the wrong syllables, the rhythm staggered and limped. The result was peculiar and not without charm, at least for a while. The folk-tales I knew well, but now I heard them anew in the dreamy distortions of her weary, garbled English. Sometimes the drift of the story became so foggy that I had to interrupt her and ask her to go back to some landmark still showing valiantly above the miasma of misplaced sounds. She was not offended and repeated herself with as little clarity as before.

All the while the husband laid down his slow lines. He said

nothing beyond a request for a slight turn of the head, or a tilt of the chin. He worked patiently, well-used to the fidgeting of young sitters. There was resignation in everything he did, in the strokes of pencil or chalk or crayon, in the deliberate gathering up of material at the end of the session, in the formality of each day's leave-taking, a handshake and a hint of a bow, and then the two Czechs, in tandem in work as in life, stepped carefully into the perspiring streets, her arm in his, his soft fine hair flopping a little with each solemn stride.

'I don't know how they survive,' said my mother, when the portraits were finished and paid for, and the Czechs departed for the last time, as composed as ever, but permitting themselves the valedictory of a wan smile and a little click of the heels. 'What will they live off in the future, when all of us are gone?'

★

That, too, was the question puzzling my father. In the great hollow halls of the Secretariat, under the whirr of the fans, he was trying to find an answer, not for the Czechs or others blown in by mischance, but for all of us in the family of the Indian Army.

My father's dark eyes, ringed with fatigue, made a mute appeal to the departing gods of certainty and order. The calmest of men when the pieces of life fitted easily he was jolted and shocked by fractured plans. His temper became unreliable. He was always stiff with children but now his stiffness creaked. And goodness knows our conduct was hard to endure. Too often playfulness turned to snarling and scrapping and banging the furniture about like a couple of washed-up comics whose act had gone wrong, gone mean and vindictive. We began to fight grimly, with all the venom of young animal natures. The howls and tears transfixed our mother. I saw her stand – not that I cared – with her hands over her ears and her eyes squeezed shut. In an angry despair she reported the fights to her husband. 'Do something, for goodness' sake, you're their father,' she pleaded before flouncing off to a neutral room. Father was very stern with threats and warnings, but he would not hit a child.

Then one day I cheeked him too far. He collared me and rushed me to their bedroom and aimed a few brisk blows to my bottom with a long-handled hairbrush. Immediately, my mother came running, wild-eyed, tears springing forth to mix with my hot tears of anger. 'How could you, you brute?' she wailed, scooping me out of his perjured hands and slamming the door behind her. My father beat a retreat with as much dignity as he could muster. The family, always a puzzle to him, was another institution that did not meet his canons of rationality. Settling into his favourite chair he barricaded himself behind the yellow cover of another Gollancz crime novel.

We were waiting for something, all of us in our different ways. Some crackle in the air, some electric jumpiness, was stretching nerves. What was it? Naturally, grown-ups did not confide in young boys. And in any case my father was a man hemmed in by reticence and caution. He kept secrets between himself and the office. His way of doing things did not change, just became heavier and more deliberate. In better times he liked to sing and he had a good ear but a booming untrained voice – a barrelhouse baritone. He would set up a lusty bawling in the bath, humming tunes from Offenbach, or bouncing through the lyrics of Gilbert and Sullivan (he knew several of the Savoy Operas by heart). But now there was silence in the bathroom.

I got it into my head that the event towards which we were all stumbling was the victory parade for VJ Day – the celebration for the defeat of Japan and the final end to the war. There was a buzz of preparation through February into early March of 1946. Scaffolding for temporary stands was going up along the length of King's Way. My brother and I, living so close, were often on hand to keep an eye on progress and to get in the way of workers. The incomplete structure made a fine gymnasium for jungle leaps and swings. Tarzan was well-known to us and Johnny Weismuller, he of the royal mane of hair and the swelling pectorals, was our hero. The days were radiant, the weather as comfortable as it ever gets in Delhi. After our work-out we liked to strip, sometimes down to nothing, and take a plunge in the shallow ornamental ponds of the processional way, from which we emerged with hollering policemen on our tails, taking half-hearted swishes with their *lathis* discreetly to our rear, as if shooing petulant geese.

When the day came – 7 March – everyone agreed that it was a notable *tamasha*, a fine celebration. There, on the saluting base, was victory-through-empire made manifest. Viceroy Wavell, that blunt little warrior, with suffused face and massed medals held himself rigid for two hours of marching pomp, with tanks and big guns clanking by. Commander-in-Chief Auchinleck cast an affectionate eye on *his* men of the Indian Army, the dogsbodies of far-flung triumphs so unimaginably distant – in Mesopotamia, in the Western Desert, in Sicily and Italy, in Burma – from Dogra hill-village or Tamil seaside shanty. Later, sitting on the ground in the midst of soldiers and holding a folded chapati in his right hand, Auchinleck gave his troops their *burra khana*, their great feast.

In the evening fireworks invaded the heavens – haloes of light, starbursts, sky etchings, multicoloured washes of brightness flushing the monuments of Lutyens – 'in the true Moghul style'.

Thus I remember it. But when I have read about it I see something extra, a more sombre picture. The fighting men marched but Congress boycotted the parade, holding a large counter-demonstration in the Old City. As rockets wooshed and zoomed around India Gate, rioters set the Town Hall on fire; then amid the other explosions guns spat in earnest, and rioters fell dead or wounded. From the India Office in London the Pethick-Lawrence commission had flashed through orders for a rushed constitutional change that Wavell could not be trusted to carry out. Mountbatten, the smooth snake in the constitutional grass, had arrived in India and was biding his time, making the awe due to royalty, a breezy sailor's charm and a compliant wife work for him.

In his pocket he had Wavell's dismissal and the last orders for British India.

★

Was it part of the VJ Day celebrations, the production of *Macbeth* that the British in Delhi put on? Proof that we too could go beyond bombast and uniforms and compete artistically with *Fauji Dilkush Sabha*, the Indian version of our ENSA troop entertainment, that was enrapturing native sepoys with lusty comedies and scenes from the *Ramayana* and the decorous litheness of dancing-girls? In any case, our theatricals were taken seriously, and my brother was chosen amid much competition to play the son of Macduff. For a while he was too preoccupied to quarrel, mouthing lines as he walked in tight circles around our bedroom floor. 'Thou liest,' he muttered, 'thou shag-hair'd villain.' It still didn't sound quite right. I sat on my bed with my knees up, watching with something between jealousy and wonder.

The performances were in the open air. The night I attended, clutching my mother's hand, the sky was dark velvet, as soft as swaddling clothes, pinned with diamond stars. It was very warm; people were rustling programmes, fanning themselves, women lifting skirts from the clammy cling of the chairs. But my concentration hardly wavered. Entranced, I awaited the moment – Act IV, Scene ii.

What was this? This was family, between mother and son. Survival was the issue. I listened carefully.

'And what will you do now? How will you live?'

'As birds do, mother.'

'What! with worms and flies?'

'With what I get, I mean; and so do they.'

'Poor bird! thou'dst never fear the net nor lime, /The pit-fall nor the gin.'

'Why should I, mother? Poor birds they are not set for. /My father is not dead, for all your saying.'

I was amazed. Did this speak to us intimately? Then I was frightened, seeing my father, and yet not seeing him. No, no, this was nothing – play-acting – surely we would go on. Nothing had come to an end, despite the marching men, the fireworks, the frown on Father's face, the dull steps, the irritability. Shortly, we would leave Delhi, sip no more the polluted water.

Some part of me wanted to cry out, with the First Murderer, 'Let it come down.'

Blue Hills of the South

ISTORY IN NORTH India was beginning to be written in chapters of riot and violence. Dead bodies made brutal statements. Karachi, Poona, Cawnpore, Allahabad, other places less well-known, were turning into cities with too many reasons for tears. In Calcutta and West Bengal a Muslim-declared *hartal*, or general strike, met furious Hindu resentment. In two nights of communal convulsion, how many killed? A police estimate was 5,000. Such a press of maddened people, emotions raw to the nerve-ends, willing slaughterers with so many to kill.

But this violent din reverberated far away from my young consciousness. Distant perturbations made no more noise for me than the movement of continents, the first winds of the monsoon, or the crumbling of empires. On the whole, we carried our own ease and security with us wherever we went. Calmly we stood on Delhi station under a cliff of luggage, waiting while a monster locomotive, with giant wheels and covered with a labyrinth of pipes and tubes, fussed itself into order, flooding the already foul air with a smother of steam and soots from low-grade coal. My father had been posted from Delhi back to his own Indian Army Division stationed in the Deccan. We were heading south.

The south starts at the line of the Vindhyas, or thereabouts. Loosely connected ranges of hills, west to east, close off the southern peninsula from the great plains of the north, and here the Aryan invaders stopped. The plains of the big northern rivers gave them enough territory to chew on for a long moment of history. Later, the Aryans did penetrate through the breaches of the hills into the sea-girt triangle of the peninsula, going as far as the tip of Cape Comorin and taking Brahmanism, the vedanta and their characteristic caste system with them. And with the roll of time the Muslims followed them, dotting the southern land with Islamic kingdoms, principalities, robber baronies and pirate castles.

But all the time the south resisted in its own supple, subtle way, keeping its own Dravidian languages, being deliberately behind the times, doing things in its own backhanded manner. Five prohibitions, wrote the early lawgivers, distinguish the people of the south: eating with one who is not initiated, dining with women, eating food kept overnight, marrying the daughter of a maternal uncle, and marrying the daughter of a paternal aunt. Life was intimate, private, undemonstrative, convivial, encircled by old pacts and runes, hidden enough to make the southern historian wince at the paucity of his material. The story of the north was spectacularly well-documented by Aryan records; the ancient southlands were largely silent. So many ferments important to future civilization began in North India. By the time they had flushed down to the south they registered little more than a mild after-taste, accommodated with tact or with sensible resignation, accepted like the tropical sun on the backs of the native fishermen. Things that could not be avoided. The south countered dangerous and novel explosions in society with longevity, endurance, assimilation. The people were the root from which the peculiar variety of the Indo-Aryan stock grew. 'The scientific historian of India,' wrote one member of that fraternity, 'ought to begin his study with the basin of the Krishna, of the Kaveri, of the Vaigai, rather than with the Gangetic plain, as has been now long, too long, the fashion.'

Lacking facts the traveller to the south entered a world of murmurs, dreams, partial memories, conjectures, reticence, and finally silence.

For four days or so our railway carriage became our inviolable shell. We camped in there in a safe dimness, taking the measure of the world through the slatted blinds over the windows, opening the door only when it suited us. At night, the upper bunks, tipped up against the walls, were swung down and spread with bulky bedrolls in their stiff canvas covers. Meals were taken on the move. During leisurely halts at the larger stations the bearer, coming at a run from the back reaches of the train, was sent to bring tin tiffin boxes from the station restaurant. Sometimes, at a junction, the stop was long enough for us to climb down, shaking out cramped legs, and then saunter on to the restaurant. Afterwards there might be a moment for a brief stroll, sometimes bathed in scarlet sunrise, sometimes seeing dusk creep in under the wings of flying foxes. Walking about we knew that we would be called in time. The train would not depart without due warning to the white sahibs. And if haste cut short a meal, hunger was served at every wayside halt by a host of food-vendors clamouring against the windows, holding up trays of *pan* or *roti* or or samosa or bhaji, or slopping warm tea from urns into small bowls of clay. Then the engine hooted and the driving wheels slipped and gripped, long plumes of smoke or steam made ghosts of the still-shouting vendors, and slowly we were on our way.

With Delhi and the north left well behind the train twisted through the green gates of the hills, creaking up and down, and then loosened its stride onto the long sunlit spread of the Deccan, at one with its racing shadow, huffing and shoo-shooing just like a child's toy, thumping on the indifferent railbed as if to a syncopation on the tabla drums. We swayed soporifically in the privacy of our carriage-caravan, voyeurs, fleeing uncommitted across the high table-land of boulder and scrub and hard-worked earth. We were drowsy in the heat of the day, sipping from a Thermos, napping, playing I-spy from the window, counting the varieties of rib-gaunt domestic beasts. At irregular intervals the wheel-note changed, registering a sudden alarm, a slow deep hammering indicating the beginning of a bridge. Then the train eased itself gingerly over the wide dirty waters of the Wardha or the Godavari or the Krishna or the Pennar, cautiously stitching bank to crumbling bank over the naked backs of river-folk sounding the buff current with poles and oars and nets.

Abruptly, the tropical evening drained light from the sky. Then I slept wonderfully in the cradle of my bunk, as if rocked by the hand of the primeval nurse.

At Bangalore we paused in our journey, resting for a couple of days in a transit hostel for officers' families. In the large grounds, fat jungly plants overflowed the paths. Outrageous flowers were like splashes from the paint-pot of a tipsy god. In the dining-room, under a heavy, frayed punkah, rice was served rather than the thin breads of the north. Fruits new to me had thick horny skins, rough and blotched. Somewhere nearby a violin was being played in the South Indian manner, wailing up and down in tremulous slides, the sound strangely familiar but the musical matter utterly alien, like a human voice crying in unknown tongues. A *mridangan* drum gave a beat, small pebbles falling into the pool of a deep cave.

The people were slight and short, a companionable height for a boy. Already the great raw length of the Europeans was looking out of place, the reddened, peeling skin and tow-coloured hair set off against dark faces, glossy black hair and smiles suddenly switched on with the clarity of electric lights.

The sun seemed more concentrated, an unforgiving eye, glaring through folds of sticky heat. The south was welcoming us.

★

Our destination was the hill town of Coonoor in the blue hills of the Nilgiris. The problem of education had arisen once more. Needing something more regular than the episodes of eccentric or indifferent schooling in the north my brother and I were being sent to a boarding school in the hills for the children of the Raj, a small enclave of white boyish faces that studiously followed the pattern and ethos of the British 'prep' school. We British were always backing away towards some atavistic line of defence, some bolt-hole from which we could scan the territory in safety, without giving ourselves away.

After the sudden glimpse of Bangalore, with all that I could surmise about a new slant to life in a new-looking country, the rest of the journey to the Nilgiris felt like a retreat. At the foot of the mountains, at Mettuppalaiyam, we transferred to the undersized train that made the 17-mile ascent to Coonoor. A little tubby engine struggled uphill, pushing a few carriages, each one as intimate as a closet, up the rack-and-cog railway. The effort looked incongruous, as if reluctant elephants were being shoved backwards into steep places where they did not want to go. From time to time the engine stopped and panted, breathing heavily out over the sharp-edged ghat and the pale, heated plain. At about 6,000 feet the train came to rest in a micro-climate so temperate and comfortable, so fanned by lazy breezes, that the British, preoccupied as always with the weather, could hardly stop talking about it.

'*Wonderful* weather,' was the greeting in the street, and with a sense of gratitude at finding such a thing in India, 'yes, another *lovely* day.'

At the head of Hulikal ravine the lower town and the bazaar huddled around Coonoor station, cramming into the niches of the hills. Hardworking rickshaws made the short climb to the upper town. Here the spacious eyries of the Raj, in stone or local brick, commanded the views like so many captains on the bridge. In this part of the town the sense of familiarity for the British was so pervasive that it must have been a work of the unconscious, since something more studied or deliberate would have stood out like a film-set. But this townscape had all the marks and tell-tales of a favourite old coat, form-hugging, weathered beyond fashion, noticed only in absence. Memsahibs in sensible laced shoes wore light cardigans against the morning air. Small pert dogs followed them on leads for a round of the shops. Sahibs buttoned tweed jackets and struck the hilly paths with stout walking-sticks. Vigorously they strode into town, enjoying once again the pleasure of a walk, having endured for too long the sweat-soaked, fly-pestered, foot-swelling weariness of the plains. Dropping down through the mottled shade of eucalyptus and Australian wattle they heard the town cooing to them, promising the warmth of memories and the safety of home, like a nanny presiding at the nursery tea.

A shop window showed a row of Arthur Ransome's *Swallows and Amazons* books. The barber's shop displayed the proper candy-striped pole. A tea-shop served Huntley & Palmer biscuits. A poster for film-night at the Club offered Douglas Fairbanks in cutlass-wielding splendour. Sim's Botanical Gardens respectfully solicited a visit. The ride by charabanc to Ootacamund was recommended. Sunsets seen from the mountain road were particularly fine.

We had arranged accommodation a little beyond the upper town. Going by broad domed pastures of hummocky grass, looping around clefts and gullies thick with stunted trees, we followed a well-kept road bordered with heliotrope and fuchsia to the geranium-scented lawns of Uplands. Here the owner, Mrs Sharp-Smith, spun out her widow's evening surrounded by the spoil and booty of a hundred years of tight-fisted imperial commerce, all packed into an elegant colonial bungalow. Amid the fabulous knick-knacks in silver and bone-china, the boule cabinets and the tapestries, the silk Persian rugs and the figures in marble or terracotta, the old matriarch surveyed her domain, propped against the many pillows of her day-bed, feeling the after-warmth of successful enterprise flow in through the french windows from her wide acres beyond.

At the end of the cascade of well-trimmed grass, under tall eucalyptus trees, stood a small square bungalow, converted from what used to be servants' quarters. We were permitted to rent this little house.

★

The man was rubbing long bony hands. The flesh on his face was pulled back to the skull. His voice was hoarse and deep, suggesting the security of the grave.

'Yes, dear lady,' he was saying, 'our syllabus is *very* carefully tailored to the needs of schooling back home. And my wife, of course, *personally* looks after the welfare of the boys while they are here at Highlands.'

My father had returned to soldiering in the Deccan. We were about to join the attenuated little flock of sixteen boys, the boarders at Highlands School. While the headmaster, Mr Mitchell, was reassuring my mother with a tour of the premises, I was trying to take stock of our new situation.

The school was poised high on the long slope of Tiger Hill. The low building was designed in the familiar colonial style, with light, airy rooms opening straight onto a field of rough-cut grass. The world appeared to slope away from the school, the eye tumbling off the steep escarpment and floating free over the plains far below. Oblivious to the view a small group of boys was horsing around on the grass, riding piggy-back and trying to unseat each other, like medieval knights in the lists. These boys eyed us newcomers without enthusiasm. So far as I could see, there was only one Indian boy in their midst.

There was a melancholy about the place – an abode of vanishing memories. The numbers in the school could never have been large, the buildings were too small, but now the whole school – the few boys and the fewer staff – sensed a tailing down, approaching a rick in the smooth flow of England's destiny. Dwindling band though we were, Mr Mitchell did his best to leave us undismayed. He spoke much of 'us', meaning the whole history of the British in India. He would not demean the 'natives' – certainly not, excellent people – but in all honesty what was there in the Nilgiris before 'we' came? The pastoral, tattooed Todas with their buffalo-haunted rituals, or the shy, magic-wielding Kurumbas of the woodlands? A few lonely forts, part of a defensive line formed by Hyder Ali and his son Tipu Sultan? A Roman coin, they say, was found in Ootacamund.

All that changed. Tipu was defeated and killed at Seringapatam in 1799, and his kingdom passed into the possession of the East India Company. Lowland Englishmen, forever seduced by mountains, climbed into the hills, in search of flora and fauna, and remarked on the sweet balm of the climate. Mr John Sullivan, the Collector for the Company at Coimbatore, arrived in 1819. Perhaps he saw the hillsides of *Strobilanthes* in bloom, a vast and vivid blue that drowned the hills and then died, as they did once every seven years. He became an enthusiast and propagandist for *Nilagiri* – the 'Blue Mountains' – of the local tribes. In 1827 a sanatorium for the Europeans of the Madras Presidency was established at Ootacamund, a few miles uphill from Coonoor. This became the chief town of the mountains. Governor Lushington himself began to take a keen interest. 'It will be the glory of Mr Lushington's government,' wrote a contemporary, 'without extravagant hyperbole, that he introduced Europe into Asia, for such are his improvements in the Nilgiris.'

No one questioned what Europe was *doing* in Asia in the first place. And as to the improvements, 'just look around,' said our headmaster, gesturing grandly in every direction. Out of 'our' sense of responsibility, and hard work, came a worthy legacy. Look at those very extensive tea and coffee plantations on the lower slopes of the hills. The cinchona trees, the source of quinine, introduced from South America under the patronage of Sir Clements Markham. Berkshire pigs established and successfully crossbred with a Chinese variety. A Western stock of horses raised at Masnigudi, to the joy of the local hunt. Low-grade gold-bearing ores mined in the 1880s (a dubious enterprise leading to the boom and bust of a speculative bubble). A cordite factory at Wellington. More cheerfully, and with greater profit, four breweries established in the towns of the hills, and one distillery at Aravanghat. Even the ever-present eucalyptus and wattle trees were a gift from the Raj, being introduced from Australia to replace forests denuded by the great building boom after Governor Lushington had done his work.

But most dear to Mr Mitchell's heart was Ootacamund, queen (as people told each other much too often) of India's hill stations. The litany of its rich features brought a smile to the headmaster's face: Government House, St Stephen's Church, Charing Cross, the Civil Courts in redbrick gothic, good old Spencer's store, the Club (where the game of snooker was invented) and the Gymkhana Club, Fernhill and Aranmore (the summer palaces of maharajahs), and the stuffy old mansion of the Nizam of Hyderabad. On the fringes of the town, in invigorating mountain air, were the polo ground and cricket field in Hobart Park, and the golf course sharing Wenlock Downs with the followers of the Ootacamund Hunt, ardent pursuers of the tricky hill-jackal with hounds brought specially from England. Even the tall surrounding peaks of Doda Betta, Elk Hill and Snowdon, each over 8,000 feet, were somehow blessed, standing watch above carefree and glorious Ooty.

Mr Mitchell had the eye of vision but the daily grind of teaching seemed beneath the dignity of a headmaster. Most of our lessons were taken by Mr Jones, a middle-aged bachelor of great experience whose impassive face refused to be surprised by any foible of youth. He would rap the desk and quell even the most turbulent spirit with a stony, prolonged stare. Then the rebel would look down in confusion and Mr Jones would allow himself a fleeting grin, briefly revealing tobacco-stained teeth. He was a polymath who appeared to grasp the elements of all subjects, at least at our low level, and I wondered even then at his presence in this outpost of scholarship. Looking back I recall that he was an MA of London, not Oxford or Cambridge, and perhaps that had condemned him to colonial drudgery. Snobbery drove as many to India as did poverty. Or perhaps the spring of youth had carried him tumultuously to foreign adventure. If so, nothing of that rashness was apparent now. Was he content with his exile? For us students there was no way of telling. He gave nothing away. He served. That was enough.

We wore a uniform, prickly shorts, long socks, and gathered each morning for a communal prayer, eyes respectfully cast down before our undemanding Anglican God. The moment was more convention than worship and easily embraced Adi, our one Indian boy, who came from a rich Parsi family. He did not object and murmured his pieties with the rest of us. Though there were too few students for proper team games, hack-abouts on the bumpy grass were encouraged, loosely patrolled by the headmaster who permitted any sporting sin except swearing and loss of temper. Often we were called together for long hikes, where instruction was still mixed with recreation. We panted through dappled forest on steep hillsides with eyes open for unusual plants or geographical formations, or for the scuttering of some small beast in the undergrowth. Out of breath we paused at the clifftop, plucking guavas, while Mr Jones explained that from this height we could see exactly 109 miles in the direction of Madurai. He had worked it out by trigonometry, which seemed to me, having not reached that far in the textbook, a very smart magic.

In the evening, we sat at two long trestle tables, poking at sweet potato and mung beans and purple vegetables that we did not much like. Before bed we stripped in the dormitory and ran naked to the bare cement bathhouse where Indian servants filled small zinc tubs with hot water carried in old jerry-cans from an outside boiler. We splashed and larked, but once when the horse-play got out of hand Mr Mitchell beat the lot of us without distinction, incensed not so much by the mess (the servants would clear that up) but by the wanton waste of soap, which was an item provided for us from the school inventory.

★

The Hindu kingdom named after Vijayanagar, the 'City of Victory', one of the ancient realms of South India, had developed, bloomed luxuriously, then lay broken and abandoned on the south bank of the Tungabhadra River. After many years of neglect, the riot of exuberant monumental architecture lapsed in rural peace into a state of stones wrapped in the roots of banyan trees.

This old kingdom was the touchstone of southern Indian glory, the demonstration of what had been and the lament for what was no longer. The ruins were almost forgotten, but the story somehow entered, in a manner as fragmented and incomplete as the buildings themselves, into our dormitory tales. Where had these tatters of storytelling come from? Was it Adi the Parsi, a worldly and knowledgeable boy rather older than most of us, who had started us going? In garbled accounts after lights-out, in low voices while the scents of the Indian night drew us back from sleep, we went in search of the fabulous, perhaps with the same lazy drift and insecure geography that the Arthurian knights had gone wandering into mystic country in their pursuit of Sarras and the Grail.

With wonder and inaccuracy we lost ourselves in stories of a city more extensive than the eye could reach, of temples so large and splendid that gods themselves could walk there at ease, of palaces with so many rooms that some were never visited or mapped, of an elephant house like celestial lodgings, of a king dressed in white silk with flowered embroidery encrusted with jewels who never wore the same garment twice. We spoke of riches and cruelty, of diamonds as big as a fist, of gold weighed by the half-ton, of criminals suspended by a meat-hook under the chin, of widows burnt abominably in the practice of suttee. We boasted, as if they were our own, of armies blotting out the ground with semi-naked warriors, of battle-elephants made drunk before fighting, of embassies escorted by 50,000 horsemen. Most of all, we whispered about women, beings almost unknown to us, but whose forms were beginning to break into our dreams, hopes and delirium. In ill-formed imagination we saw kings with too many wives and innumerable concubines, temples with thousands of dancing-girls said to give services of a lascivious kind that we could not as yet name. Night-long feasts and entertainments reeled through our minds where horses and elephants also danced and eunuchs discreetly threaded the throng with messages of assignation and love.

Exhausted by the mystery of a grandeur and an excess that seemed to me superhuman, I fell back at last into the relief of sleep.

Reality, I learnt later, was richer than dreams. Contemporary chronicles by Domingo Paes and Fernão Nuniz, Portuguese travellers who visited the great king Krishnadeva Raya at Vijayanagar in the 1520s, pictured a genial megalomania, a baroque extravagance, that outdid anything in Europe. Louis XIV, the Sun King, was a stammering princeling compared to Krishnadeva. This plump man with marks of smallpox on his face, wrote Paes, was 'the most feared and perfect king that could possibly be'. He was a cheerful soul who drank a pint of sesame oil at daybreak, then lifted weights and wrestled and practised sword-play until the oil was sweated out of him. He had a merry disposition, but beware of his rage!

It was clear that this king operated on a different human level, raising up on the foundation of his absolutism a social, intellectual and moral structure dizzy in its extent, stupefying in the richness of its detail, and most daring in its claim to power over things of the earth and things of the mind.

Domingo Paes stood on a hill in Vijayanagar and could not see where the city ended. And who could divine the limits of the king's wishes? Even the most ordinary of his desires, the thirst for conquest, seemed to stretch the possibilities of human accomplishment. When, in 1520, Krishnadeva marched against Adil Shah of Bijapur, and they met at Raichur on the bank of the Krishna River, the army of Vijayanagar numbered 703,000 infantry, 32,600 cavalry and 551 elephants. Numerous camp followers brought this host to over a million. Should we believe the reliable Nuniz? That was nothing, wrote the equally reliable Paes, at a pinch the king could raise even two million.

This was in the South Indian tradition, an ingrained way of glory. Former dynasties – Chalukyas, Pallavas, Pandyas, Cholas, Hoysalas, even the Muslim Bahmanis – with lesser means had still acted up to the hilt. 'Accept this purse of gold,' said an earlier king of Vijayanagar to a Persian ambassador, 'since we may not eat together, this is the feast I give you.' Largeness of the soul mattered. It was demonstrated by great works, great ambition, great display, great success, but also great waste and loss, and great falls. The mere human was expendable (the life of man, in any case, had but a short run), but acts and spirit endured. The courtiers of Bahmani wore jewels on the instep of their slippers, but the chances of their lives lay hidden in the hands of the sultan. The jewels still glint in the annals of time, the names of the courtiers are utterly lost.

Highlands School taught us well. I learnt much about England, though I lived thousands of miles away. I read Harrison Ainsworth and Rafael Sabatini, and knew something about Danelaw, and began my acquaintance with Euclid and my long battle with algebra (how strange that we were never told of India's gift of the zero to the world of numbers). I kicked footballs here and there, and whacked a cricket ball cross-batted into the bushes of the hillside. I stood and held out my hand stoically when I had broken the rules, then jammed my stinging palms into my armpits, trying not to blubber. But something appeared to be missing from this education. In odd moments, when faced with the thundering verities on the blackboard, I thought wistfully of the wild tales of Vijayanagar, so preposterous and heart-lifting, that stumbled mouth to mouth in the untrustworthy whispers of the dormitory.

Listening to them I, a boy of the Raj, grew into something more than an English boy. I became a participator, however remote, in a stranger, larger humanity.

ELEVEN

In Churchill's House

LORD RAMA, IT was well known, had visited this site on the bank of the Musi, in the days when the river ran free and many gods roamed the land. Some miles to the north and east, in the scrabble of calcareous rock and lowering boulders, was the hill of Kadam Rasul which, legend had it, bore an imprint of the Prophet's foot. Midway between these holy places was the camp of the interlopers, the 20 square miles of the Secunderabad cantonments where, since before the days of the Mutiny, the soldiers and the allies of the Raj kept watch. They were always in readiness, and among the stratagems they used was the trick of the old game: divide and rule. In those days they could discern the face of the enemy, ever-changing though he was. But now, it hardly mattered who was friend and who was foe. Well-wishers and implacable opponents alike were agreed on one thing, and the message was clearly understood. It was time for the British to let go. There was no longer any room for the Raj between Lord Rama and the Prophet Mohammed.

★

In the cantonment village of Bolarum, on the outskirts of Secunderabad, my father had been assigned a house in which Winston Churchill had once lived. That was in Churchill's swashbuckling military days, in the early years of the twentieth century, when the Raj was set for the long haul, and young Churchill carried forward the interests of empire on his own jaunty shoulders. I saw a photo of him from this time – the cavalry officer's glad-rags, the insouciant chubby face beneath a regimental topee canted at a provocative angle. The face wore that expression later to be so well-known, the look of cheerful belligerence that was almost a smirk. He was surveying the imperial territory around him and approved it as right and well-founded and set to endure.

His house in Bolarum – now our house – also looked built to survive. It was a large granite bungalow, designed in what seemed to be a modification of Scottish baronial style. Two short wings flanked a massive central portion rising like a bold forehead over a long curved verandah. The roofline of rough-cut stones had a look of crenellations and defences. It was a cool, commodious house, rooms with shuttered windows and high ceilings shady against the sunlight, set well away from other houses in about half an acre of grounds. In the front were flowerbeds and a driveway of swept earth; in the back rank grass and low scrub under a few droopy trees cut off the bungalow from the servants' quarters in the far corner – a row of small hutches in cracked and weather-stained plaster, like discarded boxes for old shoes. Beyond the granite gateposts of the front entrance, holding their discipline against the wild embrace of the bougainvillaea, across a quiet unpaved road, the open space of the maidan began. This gave way to a golf course, not much used but always carefully tended, with the sandy 'browns' (the turf was too coarse and sparse for proper 'greens') as closely combed as regimental haircuts.

Then, beyond this, at some undefined point, demarcation became blurred. The shape of the present, with its insistent political and economic plans, faded into the ancient elements of the countryside. Sight strained against a vast expanded sky that gave the eye no place to rest, no surety of an end.

When the cooler months came to the Deccan we travelled from the Nilgiris to rejoin our father in Secunderabad. The family was united, but in what sense, and for what end?

The trappings and authority of his command imposed a routine upon my father. Military orderliness kept uncertainty at bay. In the morning his staff-car arrived at seven, before the heat of the day. His tall thin frame, doubled over the bloomer-like khaki tropical shorts, eased into the back seat, and then my father left without fuss or comment, as he had been doing all the years of my young life. He returned at lunch but soon retired for a siesta, lying in pyjamas under the old wheezing fan (my father was an excellent sleeper, with a smoker's tendency to snore). In late afternoon he went back to his office to round off the working day. The burden was not very heavy. When he bathed before dinner, often I would hear his croaky baritone bouncing out of the tin tub.

Dinner was the important family moment in the day, almost formal, for which we boys were expected to be on good behaviour, washed and combed and with our buttons done up. The table was laid on white linen, our napkins rolled in silver rings. Beside each place was a Japanese lacquered finger-bowl, deep glossy black with a gold interior. Sami, the bearer, had changed from his working day-clothes into full formal dress – long white tunic with a broad cummerbund in the regimental colours, *pugree* and stiff white turban again showing the regimental colours. The house-boy – the *chokra* – carried the trays of food a dozen paces from the little outside kitchen (no more than a hut on blocks with a cooker fashioned from two cubes that had been kerosene cans) to the small back verandah. This was Sami's domain, where my father's boots and shoes lay in a row and his Sam Browne belt hung on the wall, all buffed to a mirror-like finish. In the corner, below the full shelf of glasses, the bulky GEC refrigerator kicked suddenly into a spasm of throbs.

When Sami served the food, a solicitous ghost at the table (I had grown used to servants), I recall now the competence and quiet dignity of the man. He had worked hard in the service of the Raj. To be bearer in the family of a senior officer was his reward. He had no conception of inferiority, nor of disloyalty to India. Did he think of himself as 'Indian'? He told me once that he was from the Western Ghats, on the edge of the Deccan. Most likely a Maratha. But I see now just a man proud of his place, his skill, his experience. Deftly he judged the demands of the dinner, that the main dish should not get cold while the soup was being drunk but should be kept warm on the charcoal hot-plate on the back verandah. When he served, a plate with a crest was placed just so, with the crest four-square under the eye. When he moved he was there, and then he was gone, bare feet with slippers kicked off by the back door making no sound on the matting of the floor. If there was laughter at table at some childish crack – I was something of a little comedian in those carefree days –

I saw Sami turn quickly away to hide a grin. He would never be impertinent, but he was human, and he spoke excellent English.

The dinner, of course, was firmly British. Nothing to set the gastric juices running. Soup, thick or thin, but generally brownish in colour; chicken, or an egg dish, or a piece of tough meat; vegetables with potatoes (no rice); fruit, or a custard pudding. Only in the matter of vegetables and fruit were the infinite resources of India brought into play, lady's fingers or aubergine or sweet potato or *dal* sneaking in cautiously in the place of sprouts or cabbage. After dinner, my mother liked an English chocolate, its surface under the wrapping turning ashy grey in the tropical heat.

After some months in Bolarum, when Sami's son Rahul had taken us in hand and shown us something of Indian ways, my brother and I supplemented this stodgy fare with spicy Indian messes eaten with fingers and folded chapati in the lee of the cookhouse or squatting on the beaten earth in front of the servants' quarters. I noticed then that the leftovers from our family table, however plentiful, were thrown to the dogs and chickens.

★

The ladies had come to the house. Some of them I knew by sight – Bunty and Audrey and Halcyon and Begum. It was the mah-jong morning and my mother's turn to entertain. The 'girls' (for so they often called themselves) were in good humour, lighthearted and casually dressed in slacks or sporting clothes. One wore a loose, colourful turban, fashionable in Hollywood films, another wore jodhpurs and boots ready for an afternoon's riding. Only Begum – lovely, dark-eyed, slinky Begum, young wife of an Indian officer – was carefully dressed in a sari with her face made up to show off her striking features.

My mother was excited. This was her moment. She had discussed the shape of the morning with Sami, giving her orders, her voice rising at the anxious points. Was the silver coffee-pot polished? And the sugar-bowl? The best china cups, naturally. Biscuits, of course – a good selection from the big round tin. Cigarettes? Make sure both the silver and the sandalwood box were well-filled. And have sherry and glasses ready in case the session went on to lunch. Wear the cummerbund, the regimental colours look so nice. And no need to keep popping in, we'll tinkle the bell if we want you.

Though I knew nothing about mah-jong I liked to watch it very much. So long as I was quiet I could stay in the background nibbling a biscuit and pretending to read. But the game had my attention. The pattern of play looked rich but obscure, and the pieces were so handsome. My mother had a fine old set in ivory, with bold Chinese characters. When the game began the contest looked complicated to me, both cunning and free-spirited according to the pressures. Sometimes a lady would lounge back in her chair, almost dreaming, cigarette smoke drifting into narrowed eyes. Then one would pounce, springing forward intent upon some artful strategy. Mostly, I kept my eye on the pretty Indian lady. 'O gosh,' she would say with a radiant smile when things were going well, and in sticky moments, 'My dear, *so* aggravating.' From time to time she smoked, puffing nervously, as if caught in a naughty act. I noticed she would say 'Blighty' for England.

Bets were made in tiny amounts – annas not rupees – just to keep the play slightly daring.

In the pauses for coffee social events were co-ordinated and intently anatomized.

'On Saturday there's the cocktail party at the General's house. I take it that we're all going?'

'They say some Indian big-wig is expected – such a bore really – and of course one hardly knows what to wear on those occasions. A pretty dress might look too frivolous – we're all on our best behaviour now! – but formality is so dull.'

'It's all right for you, Begum, you always look so elegant in your sari. And your skin looks so *well* out of doors. Poor us, we need all the creams we can get.'

'To change the subject – *that* dinner in Trimulgherry! Such fun.'

'When were we last there? More than two months ago? My, how time flies.'

'But that girl, so indiscreet, and more than a little squiffy. Who was she?'

'Some box-wallah family, I gather.'

'How shaming.'

'Jim was just terrible, of course, but that's Jim.'

With the past wrung out for the moment, the future was planned. A busy round of visits ahead. An extended dinner party in instalments, a different course eaten in each household, and a mad dash to the next. 'No, be serious for a minute. Who's going to organize that? And someone had better stay sober to drive.' Then there was the fancy-dress party at the Club. 'What are we all going as? Such a shame if we all go as clowns, or witches!' (My father always went as a tramp, with stubble of burnt cork, and, a Charlie Chaplin walking-stick.) It was settled. Halcyon would co-ordinate the dinner, and Bunty find out about the fancy dress.

Suddenly it was time to go. The lady in the jodhpurs jumped up, looking at her watch. She was already late.

'Must hurry. There's this darling man waiting to give me a lesson.'

'Bye-bye,' they cried, 'toodle-oo.'

'Don't forget the Club on Sunday,' shouted my mother, waving hopefully.

After they were gone my mother was distracted. She looked a little lost. She frowned around the sitting-room, stubbing out a cigarette impatiently, almost willing some insult to her sense of good order. But Sami and the chokra, efficient as usual, had everything neat and cleared away. Lunch was already planned. Perhaps a little nap afterwards. But my mother was often too nervous, too high-strung, to sleep during the day. She didn't ride, or play tennis. She would not take a walk on the maidan – what was the point of such a tedious pastime? One wasn't *going* anywhere – and too much sun was not good for her delicate skin. She was allergic to something – pollen or dust – that brought out her urticaria.

In early evening, when the worst of the heat had gone out of the day, she would take her hat and gardening gloves and poke about in the flowerbeds, not really knowing what she was doing (though she dearly loved flowers), her actions quick and agitated but somehow inconclusive. A stab at the ground, a weed yanked out with distaste, a flower, its roots disturbed, left leaning piteously.

I followed her with a watering-can. When she pointed to the cannas I gave them a good drenching, though their thirst in the dry friable earth seemed bottomless.

★

In our own wing of the house my brother and I lived free and easy. We had our own bedroom, playroom and bathroom – a tin tub, a wooden washstand, a big square thunderbox with a contemplative view through the open outside door onto dappled shade. Between rising and bedtime in the cool, comfortable bungalow we came and went more or less as we pleased.

Despite this freedom I began to feel awkward and fretful in the house. Around me I saw a collection of unspoken rules that I was beginning to acknowledge but did not understand. Hierarchies were becoming entangled with human relations. Sami, for example, how did he stand with us? He was as careful towards us as a father, and far more available, steering us towards better sense and covering us from parental wrath. He, far better than my parents, knew what I was up to. What is more, he sympathized with adventure, however wild and foolish, and forgave the stupidities of youth. Once, late at night, when my parents were out, I gave the servants an impromptu fashion show, wrapped in a sheet. I was silly and slightly lewd, waggling a bare bottom and sketching some effeminate gestures. The cook, a bony old cadaver with a grizzled, soup-strainer moustache, was shocked. He spoke almost no English and appeared to regard working for the Raj as a necessary evil at best. Sniffling through his beaky nose he raised bloodshot eyes for judgement. Nearly every day he witnessed some obscenity, and now he was not surprised to be disgusted. But Sami was both amused and anxious. He was indulgent towards a bit of childish play-acting but anxious that all of us should not get it in the neck if my father returned suddenly. He shooed us into bed with mock severity and left chuckling.

By what right, I began to wonder, did I give this man orders, sending him here and there like a pawn on a board? The chokra, a lively youth in his late teens, dropped his eyes when he came upon us and circled around by the wall. And the sweeper, whom I saw most days emptying the thunderbox from our bathroom? In the house he was an Untouchable, a carter of ordure. But to see him outside in the grounds, slowly whisking a broom of twigs through the dust, I now saw him as an Indian, a fellow human, possessor of an autonomous life.

These perplexities were like a fog between four walls, penetrated by the hushed voices of the servants, calls from a far, unknown shore. I wanted to rush outside, to clear the air, to avoid the stringencies of the house. Nature's back was broad. Undecided questions lay more easily amid the boundlessness of the land.

It was partly a matter of climate, of course. Apart from hunger and malaria and cholera and smallpox and rickets and uncorrectable griefs, there is a sense in which children of hot lands are blessed. I, at least, plump and healthy and itching with curiosity, was graced by the large allowance of time and freedom granted me by the sun. Beyond the gate was a universe to be cracked open and savoured each day, as tasty and full of promise as a newly baked bun.

We had our bicycles. When we were not at school we dashed from the house as soon as possible and in a short time we had left behind the dusty roads of the cantonment, shaded by palmyra and date palms. We launched ourselves onto faint beaten tracks scuffed into a parched sandy ground, meandering through brushwood and rank plants, past fields of *cholam*, gram, cotton and rice, with a few tall sentinel trees standing over the rough, crouching, boulder-strewn land. In the distance scattered villages hid in groves of tamarind and cottonwood and mango and fig. Dotted around these islands of habitation, the 'tanks' – large ponds dammed and dug for the irrigation of this porous land – gleamed like pale mirrors. At certain times the fields reeked of toddy, thick juice trickling from the palms into earthenware pots left to ferment in the sun.

In the heat of the day the ringing clamour of birdsong fell away – just an occasional whirr of wings or rattle of alarm. We cycled through the marks of their territory. A store of grubs and insects impaled by the shrike on acacia thorns. A colony of pendulum-houses made by weaver birds. Out of sight, animals were at their ease, breathing deeply under shade. Only a few showed themselves by the cool of a well or waterhole. A jackal lapping quietly, leaving hardly a ripple; a disturbed hare exploding into open ground like a shot from a gun.

Once, at a deep watering-hole overhung by vegetation, where a buffalo was working a long boom, creaking a bucket in and out of the muddy water, I saw a python slip noiselessly from water to low branch, a movement as fluid as the water itself, an uncoiling of a long jewelled rope. On another occasion, swimming in a flooded *jheel*, I saw a cobra cruise by me at a distance of about a dozen feet. I was far from shore, and it was too late to panic. I stopped swimming to give a bursting heart some relief and watched, with wonder starting to overcome terror, the sinuous ease of the motion. The snake's head was held proud of the water and the hood was just a little distended, like a shawl on a king.

★

'A snake, you see a *big* snake?' Rahul, the bearer's son, was amused. Snakes were not uncommon, shy creatures that left you alone so long as you did not disturb them. Even cobras, despite the scares of Kipling's story, avoided humans if they could.

Rahul was my informant on native matters concerning flora and fauna, custom and practice. He put up with my questions but it puzzled him that I could not see what *everyone* knew. He himself had other things in mind, being about fourteen and desperate for school knowledge and improvement. Though his natural disposition was sunny and his nature kind, his delicate, handsome face creased often with worry for the future. A command of English seemed to be one of the keys to that future and Rahul was happy to trade practice in English for some information that was no mystery anyway.

But after a while he would have had enough of questions. He would begin some fast skipping steps, whirling a bamboo cane in dazzling motion, arcing above and below and side to side, covering the whole body, as Maratha warriors had done with the sword (or so Rahul said) in the days of Sivaji. To me, it looked like an act of pure joy.

★

We were at school again, the enduring penance of youth. This time, the army school was large and formal, serving all the busy cantonments of Secunderabad. But I was used by now to an eccentric and obsessive tuition from teachers on the edge of exile and I paid little attention to my new school. The learning seemed deficient and the children rowdy and idle.

If I went with any enthusiasm at all, hanging over the tailgate of the 3-ton army truck that did the school-run for our district, it was on account of the many girls in the new school. I was approaching *that* age. The phenomenon of girls made me break into sweat, projecting me onto slippery ground where I floundered about woefully. Luckily for my maladroit shyness – had I been shown favour, then what would I have done? – the pretty girls, around whom the boys stuck like swarming bees, did me the compliment of ignoring me completely. I was free to sigh inwardly without being put to the cruel test of popularity.

There was little enough in this Secunderabad schooling to please our parents. Was it not certain, and likely to be quite soon, that we boys would be translated 'home' for the great competitive battle of influence-peddling and place-hunting known as the British public school system? If this were so we must get going, obviously, on Latin. My brother, the elder, was the first victim. He was sent for weekly lessons from the only Latinist around, who was our local Catholic priest. Monsignor Jozef (his last name, being a terrible tangle of Polish syllables, was never used), the white-bearded patriarch of our Bolarum parish, seduced us each Sunday into a doze with his deep mumbles. I never did learn what quirk of clerical fate had marooned him in the bastion of his gaunt old church, set behind thorn bushes on the far edge of the maidan.

For the Latin lessons the old priest, white beard snowy between the dark soutane and the dark biretta, met us at the sacristy door. A heavy callused hand descended on my brother's shoulder and guided him relentlessly into the dungeon of scholarship while I fled into the undergrowth.

At that time I was a keen but undiscriminating collector of birds' eggs, which I stored in metal ammunition boxes commandeered for me by my father. I was attracted more by beauty than by system or rarity, and (to the benefit of rarer species) would take one pretty egg from the large clutch of a common bird rather than look for the shy or unusual specimen. In my search for eggs, the untended greenery around the isolated church was a good place to look. I had Salim Ali's *Book of Indian Birds* with me. Doubtfully, I turned the pages between the beautiful coloured plates, trying to distinguish between the common and the large green bee-eater, between the rose-ringed and the blossom-headed parakeet. Most of the time I was lost in the dazzling flutter of small brilliant birds, while from above the rascally old cons – crows, kites, vultures – monitored their chances.

When I was finished for the day I waited by the sacristy door. From within I heard a muffled thunder of verses. Monsignor Jozef, carried away into an almost forgotten Horatian world, was going far, far beyond the competence of my brother. The sonorous Latin took the priest back to the whitewashed walls of icy Polish seminaries, to the friendships of a long-lost land:

> Frater erat Romae consulti rhetor, ut alter
> Alterius sermone meros audiret honores,
> Gracchus ut hic illi, foret huic ut Mucius ille.

All gobbledegook to us! While I was outside listening to the vivid hubbub of a bulbul, my brother crept from the door, shoulders bent under misgivings. On this evidence, the academic future was likely to be hard going.

*

We were drifting apart, India and I. At a younger age, with the trust and ignorance of childhood, I had taken the extent of my desire for the limit of the world. India had indulged me. I was entirely bathed with India – my nurse, my guardian, my playground. Now, growing older and tasting a little of the sordid fruit of knowledge, I was being drawn into distinctions. Brown and white, servant and master, native and European, them and us. These labels were insinuated into the scheme of things not as reasons for condemnation or contempt, least of all for hatred, but merely as matters of fact, aids towards a clear taxonomy in the interests of social science.

Rahul, Sami's son, understood very well the unwritten protocols. He was my pal, but only up to a point. There were moments – only too easily reached – where life parted us. 'No, no,' he would say when my brother or I proposed some unthinking devilry, 'that's all right for you sahibs. Not for me.' I saw him ready for school, so eager and neat, dressed in shorts, shirt and tie with a satchel over his shoulder. Intelligent and painstaking, he was anxious about exams. He saw his future depending on grades, marks, certificates. There was nothing to fall back on.

'Please, I must go now,' he would murmer. 'That geometry. So much work, so difficult.'

At the back end of the compound, where rubbish collected under straggly trees, well away from the flowerbeds and the big shade-trees, our paths divided. I was in a hurry to get to the fridge on the rear verandah, to the cold jug of mango juice, and then to soak in a hot tub prepared for me by the unseen hand of the sweeper; he receded to the bare box among the weeds that he shared with his parents. Already he was thinking about homework, then the little house was to be swept, and the charcoal got ready for the cooking of the evening meal in the pit in the open yard.

I was moving into conformity with my own kind, though not from conscious choice. The Secunderabad cantonment was so big – all those pale faces in Bolarum, Trimulgherry, Bowanpalli, Chilkalguda, Begampett – not just the officers and families of my father's Indian Army Division but also the men and officers of British regiments. It was hard to step around that British presence. Secunderabad, a town with no history, grown up as a scruffy handmaiden to military needs, offered little. We went there to school, and on Saturdays we usually cycled in for a day by the large swimming-pool. On the hot ride from Bolarum we tried to freewheel in the slip-stream of fumes, clinging to the battered metalwork of decrepit old steam-powered, charcoal-burning buses.

On the wide apron around the pool bodies lay as thick and supine as landed fish. There was plenty of brown flesh in evidence (shading to the angry red of sunburn) but only in very few cases was that colour the natural hue of the sunbathers.

Somewhere amid the bunched bodies and the flash of spray our friend Dai was waiting for us. He was a young Welsh corporal, a bugler with a British regiment, who appeared to look on life as a superlative lark, a kind of cosmic entertainment into which we were drawn also by his energy and enthusiasm. We had met him by the pool, a tidy little man, a pocket Atlas in a brief swimsuit, with stiff carroty hair and a wide smile. He liked to wrestle in the shallows, swoosh recklessly from the water-shoot, and splat dangerously from the top diving-board among the idle floaters below. He would grab a wrist and an ankle to hurl one of us into

space. 'Hold on, boy,' he would cry, 'I'm coming to get you.'
After ducking and mauling us with rough good humour he would
haul us to the side to lie in the sun and share his soda-pop.

I see now that he was lonely and out of place and needed an outlet
for youthful good nature. Our puppy-like devotion made him grow
an inch. He counted for little in the barracks, and India at large was
uncharted land. He wanted our simple friendship. 'Come on back to
the billet,' he invited us, 'and I'll let you have a go at the bugle.
You'll like that.' We did, and so did he. He was amused by our
attempts, our burps and growls. 'Ah, you see,' he laughed, 'it's not
as easy as it looks, is it?' Then he would take the instrument and give
us a prolonged bugle-call, playing with flair but rather too fast.

In early evening, when our ways parted, he was reluctant to let us
go. What did the night have to offer him? The bazaar teased a young
man into regrettable indiscretion. 'I like these brown beggars,' he
said wistfully. 'Good lads, most of them. But it's not like the
Rhondda valley here, is it?'

★

The good-looking Indian officer was having trouble with his horse.
Tommy Masood had come visiting in his usual way, on horseback.
He had leapt the low garden wall and cleared the flowerbeds, looped
the reins around one of the pillars of the verandah, and then stomped
into the house in his beautiful boots for a drink. Several drinks. He
was merry when he arrived and cheerfully unsteady on leaving. My
mother regarded him with alarm. 'Do something, for goodness'
sake,' she whispered to her husband.

The whisper was too loud. 'Nothing to worry about, dear lady,'
said Tommy breezily. 'Been in this pickle many a time. Pretty damn
normal, I would say. Emerge triumphant every time. Just stand back
there.'

The horse did not share the rider's confidence. Its ears went back,
the haunches dropped, and the hoofs started skittering on the stones.
But Major Tommy mounted into the saddle with the soaring ease of
the mildly drunk and had the nervous beast dancing, sashaying
sideways between the verandah and the gateposts. My mother had
taken refuge on the verandah, ready to bolt in at the french window,
while my father, who had an infantry man's distrust of horses, made

soothing noises in a surprisingly high voice. I had taken the precaution of putting a low wall between me and the horse, but I was entranced by the scene.

'Not a thing to worry about, Colonel old boy,' Tommy called out loudly, sitting ramrod straight without a hair disturbed. 'Everything perfectly top hole. Just watch out for those rear hoofs, my dear fellow.'

To prove that the animal was under control he did a quick circle of the driveway, and then with the flick of the cane and a 'Whoa, *up* there' the horse rose over the wall and was away across the maidan, leaving four good hoof-marks in my mother's flowerbed.

'That damn fool, he'll break his neck one day, and probably ours as well.' My mother sniffed her disapproval. She disliked tipsiness, though she saw it often enough at parties and at the Club. Such behaviour made her wonder about the wisdom of promoting Indian officers too quickly. 'He gives us all a bad reputation,' she complained.

But my father would have none of it. A cautious man himself he admired gallant and daring behaviour even when it bordered on the reckless.

'Nonsense,' he replied. 'A fine officer, Tommy Masood, though perhaps a little wild. He'll calm down. Anyway, the horse was under control. It was just the high spirits of a cavalry man, letting off steam.'

My father was protective towards India and strenuously defended all things Indian against the easy flow of calumny that so often came from the British. He approved of Indian officers and recommended them for promotion. He liked to meet them socially. He wanted to get their take on his beloved Indian Army that was soon to be left in their hands.

One evening, when a high-ranking Indian officer was visiting on military business, my father had invited him to the Club for dinner. It was a Saturday and my father had forgotten that Club rules decreed uniform or dinner jacket for dinner on the weekend. Both father and guest were in civilian clothes. As they entered the dining-room, anxious servants tried to head them off. My father was indignant, misunderstanding the reason for rejection, thinking that it had something to do with the presence of an Indian guest not officially cleared with the Club committee. He grew bothered and he began to stutter loudly. Then it was explained to him, in a low embarrassed aside, that the trouble wasn't in the invitation. The problem was that they were *improperly dressed*.

The day was saved by a thoughtful British compromise. Father and Indian guest were permitted to dine, but their table was pushed to the far edge of the dining-room and placed behind a screen, so that other members would not be offended by the lax conduct of officers who should have known better.

Government would pass into Indian hands, certainly. But surely, the attitude was, proper forms should be maintained. There was no place, even at this moment, for slovenly or boorish behaviour.

★

In general, in our family, we went our separate ways. Parents and children lived almost as strangers in the same house, our lives mediated through the care of servants. My brother and I relied on Sami for household information.

No common interests bound us, neither sport, recreation nor hobby. Family outings were so infrequent I remember them still with a sense of surprise: an afternoon sailing on Husain Sagar, my brother and I pushed off to make shaky progress on the placid lake while our father settled himself behind a book in a little park by the perimeter road; a visit to a nawab's palace in Hyderabad (was it the Salar Jang palace, or the Jahannuma palace of Asman Jah?) where a solemn man in a garment like a frock-coat led us through vast shadowy rooms and past a stupefying number of painted lead soldiers – many battalions of infantry and cavalry, batteries of gunners, camel troops and elephant troops, Moghuls and Marathas, the soldiers of Tipu Sultan, the scarlet of the East India Company, the khaki drab of the present. I remember also all of us standing under wayside trees, my parents smoking pensively, as we watched garlanded cattle led through village streets for the Pola festival.

So it was with some astonishment that we received one night an offer from Father to accompany him to the airport very early next morning. Planes were strange business in those days, a mysterious technical magic that promised excitement and some danger. My father had been summoned to Jhansi for some high-level meeting, important enough to make flying imperative.

We rose before sun-up and went in the eerie pre-dawn hush to the lines of the Indian sepoys to rouse the *naik* – the corporal – who would drive us to the airport. The long barrack room was silent with still sleeping men, rows of dark figures on rope-strung charpoy beds, huddled under thin blankets or with limbs thrown wildly open to the night air. The naik sprang from his bed in confusion, alarmed to see in the first glimmers of the day his colonel standing by the foot of the bed in service dress uniform. The wiry dark body of the young soldier was sweaty from sleep or nerves as he hurriedly pulled on his clothes.

We drove away in silence, seeing the dullness of the cantonment with all its shabby dirt beginning to unroll in the dawn. A few men and women plodded by the road with the steadfastness of the poor. One or two men came out of the bushes adjusting their dhotis. They had just relieved their bowels by the wayside. Father was glum and preoccupied. He tugged awkwardly at his Sam Browne belt, as if it were out of place, and drummed his fingers on his leather-covered cane.

At the airstrip – the few low buildings behind a wire fence did not seem to deserve the title of airport – we dropped my father off. We all stood by the open doors of the staff-car while he finished a cigarette. He mentioned the day of his return, ordering the car for such and such an hour.

When he had finished smoking he gave us a brief handshake and turned away muttering something like, 'Well, I suppose it's just about finished now.' What did he mean? I watched him walk away towards the reception building, very much the military man, tall but not stooped, in early middle age.

TWELVE

Time's Up

THE MATRIARCH WAS dead, just short of her hundredth year. In the hot season the family, without Father, had returned to the house of Mrs Sharp-Smith in Coonoor, to occupy once again the little cottage under the swaying eucalyptus trees. But the old lady had slipped away after years of illness and decline. In her last days she had cast a long shadow over her estate. Now the hushed voices ceased whispering and curtains were drawn back in long-darkened rooms. In the drawing-room, the silk shawl like a funereal drape came off the piano, with its beautiful case of figured wood, and a halting music stumbled, for the first time in years, from the french windows.

At the end of the garden, in the little box of our cottage, we too heard the music. This was something new for me. Previously, in our helter-skelter Indian days, I had heard snatches of Gilbert and Sullivan, or perhaps Gracie Fields, on a wind-up gramophone, the needle squealing along scratches on much-travelled 78s. Or I had been momentarily entangled in the mysterious threads of an Indian *raga* coming from the bazaar. But in general, excluding the military thump and blare of the regimental bands, the Raj at home seemed to do without music.

Poking my head around the edge of the tall window I heard the inevitable *Für Elise*. The fingers, it seemed to me, were flying over the keys. I wanted to learn that legerdemain, too, to release the trembling notes. My mother made enquiries and discovered a young American, somehow adrift in south India, who taught the piano. She was an energetic woman with a fresh, open face and plenty of bounce, and she had a thoroughly up-to-date approach to the teaching of beginners. She arrived with a bulging music-case and a long slim wooden box under her arm. A space was cleared on the floor below the Sharp-Smith piano, on the faded geometry of an old Persian rug, and the wooden box, hinged along its long side, was opened up to reveal a full-sized dummy keyboard with gleaming black and white notes, able to go up and down, but silent.

On my knees on the floor I pressed down the dummy keys. The teacher called out the names and I got to know them, pressing them singly or gathering them into clumps of chords. But no voices sounded. The real piano loomed above me, bursting with unrealized music, its lid closed in resentment. On the floor my brother and I took our first steps in classical harmony.

'Please, miss,' we begged, 'couldn't we play something? Just a few little notes.'

'OK, kids,' she replied briskly, 'you'll be playing soon enough. But first let's get with these enharmonic relationships.'

Disappointed and more sullen by the minute I descended into those theoretical thickets where no notes sang. The hesitant fumbling of childish fingers might have been good enough in the India of the old days, but this scientific method pointed to the new way of the world. After a few weeks I was sick of it. I refused to enter the music room and left my brother to grapple with silence alone.

Some time later the piano was suddenly released from this modern reticence. Brazen old tunes, part of the traditional repertoire of this most democratic of instruments, disturbed the genteel quiet of the drawing-room. The daughter of Mrs Sharp-Smith, winding up her mother's estate, had summoned an auctioneer from Bangalore to arrange for the sale of the many valuable bits of property in the house. The auctioneer was almost a caricature of his type, a plump beaming fellow in waistcoat and shirtsleeves, a few strands of coarse hair dragged over his dome, reeking of cigarette smoke and bonhomie.

During the day he busied himself with long lists of objects, his grin going from ear to ear since he had hardly ever seen such a treasure trove of furniture, carpets, china, ornaments and objets d'art gathered in one house. In the evening, in great good humour, he made a cheerful assault on the piano, pounding out unvarying chords in the left hand while the pudgy fingers of the right hand twinkled through the treble with the familiar tunes of the old favourites. Sometimes he launched into the words in a pleasant light tenor, and then the ladies gathered round were bold enough to join in tremulously, even when 'Roll out the barrel' was noisily sprung upon them.

With the lots catalogued, the jolly man departed, waving a sweaty hand. He left, in the sombre and fragile household, a memory of bold zest that slowly receded like the smile of the Cheshire Cat. Later, my mother told me that many things of heart-breaking beauty and unknown value were knocked down for a trifle and snapped up by questionable hands. Many small things were stolen. Times were getting rough, the old certainties of property were slipping. A collection so laboriously put together from all the corners of the East, the fruits of empire (some of it ill-gotten perhaps, but always selected with taste and discrimination), rested on the stability of the old order of the Raj. Mutability threw the collection to the winds, and in the emerging India, struggling with its fate, who cared where such things landed?

Months later, just before we left India, news came to my mother in Secunderabad of a tragedy at Uplands in Coonoor. Mrs Sharp-Smith's daughter, herself elderly and choosing to stay on in the echoing house that had been for so long her family home, was surprised in the night by thieves. There were cries, panic, blows that were too hard for an old lady, which killed her. She ended where she had been born, a white face in an eastern land she thought belonged to her. It was reported that the thieves, when they were caught, protested that they had been frightened, as if by a ghost, a hag-faced spirit of the night. They struck out blindly. They had not known that the house was still occupied. They thought it was a relic of the departing Raj, a place from which something useful might be salvaged.

★

Back in our house in Bolarum, when did I know we would finally have to leave India? The thought came stealthily, a rumour more than clear knowledge, a matter of feeling more than of words. A creeping melancholia. The midnight hour chosen as auspicious by the astrologers – 14 August 1947 – had come and gone. Independence, to sighs of amazement, had truly arrived. Mr Nehru, speaking after the moaning of a conch-horn, had been in his element.

'No doubt about it,' my father told me later, 'Nehru carried it off splendidly. Plenty of old-fashioned rhetoric in the grand manner. Honed by reading Pitt or Macaulay and by pleasant memories of university days at Cambridge. But very much in tune with the educated Hindu mind, which has a feeling for cosmic vastness without being able quite to put a finger on the perils of the moment. But everything was put in question by the absence of Gandhi. Where was he? He was the most important man. His absence was ominous, a question mark, a ghost at the feast.'

Gandhi was at his ashram in Calcutta from where he spoke to a foreign newspaperman. 'I have no message to give on independence,' he said, 'because my heart has dried up.'

I watched my father wither a little, too. He was forced to witness the break-up of the unified Indian Army, the one disciplined organization that gave him hope for comity and understanding in the sectarian bitterness of the new India where partisans chopped up opponents with fiendish enthusiasm. Mountbatten, both dreamer and schemer, had hoped that the divided land – now India and Pakistan – would accept a common army, at least for a transitional period. A forlorn hope, torn to bits by both sides. Regiments with a history of 200 years and more, in which Afghans and Baluchis and Jats and Sikhs and Dogras and Rajputs and Bengalis and Tamils and many more had rubbed shoulders easily enough, were dismembered. Baluchis and Pathans and Punjabi Muslims marched north and west; Rajputs and some Bengalis and Tamils went south or east. Sikhs, across whose ancestral lands the partition went, knew themselves only to be Sikhs. Before, all had been colleagues in arms. Now they were rivals, potential foes, bearing the load of nationalism.

My father, anticipating the inevitable exodus of British officers, wanted to transfer to the British Army. But he was just over the permissible age limit, though he was not yet forty-four. I saw my parents working hard to turn their minds towards England, putting behind them the habit and expectation of their adult years. Plans had to be made for life in a far land they did not know. Prospectuses for strange-sounding English schools began to arrive in the post. I looked at pictures of sleek little manikins trying to appear happy in blazers and shorts. To me, they looked revoltingly complacent and tidy. My mother began to leaf through back numbers of *The Lady*, pondering what spot in the cloud-damped landscape of England might suit us best.

★

In the years of his retirement, when my father's recollection was suffused with the sunset glow of Indian memories, I asked him what he thought of Karl Marx's opinions on the history of the Raj. He said he had never read them. Though he was a long-standing Labour supporter, my father drew political allegiance more from instinct and the heart than from social or political theory. In the General Strike of 1926, when he was a young lance-corporal in the Coldstream Guards, he had marched with his company to Victoria Park in Hackney, to the poor man's town in the East End of London. They settled in to stay, put up tents, dug latrines, posted sentries, looked steely and warlike. They had instructions to counteract 'the forces of riot and disorder'. The exceedingly well-bred Guards officers, swishing their swagger sticks, seemed keen on a confrontation. The company was issued with live ammunition. Was it the intention to shoot fellow-countrymen? Strikers whose sin it was to ask for work and a living wage? My father's disgust stayed with him for the rest of his life. To him, politics was a simple matter of fairness and justice, and he needed no continental scaffolding of theory built by Marx on Hegel and Feuerbach. Despite his experience and reading my father had never quite overcome the innate anti-intellectual prejudice of the insular English.

But I looked up the passages from Marx for him, and out of politeness he read them.

'Well, there's some food for reflection there,' he told me, 'but it's all a bit beyond my simple mind. I'll give you my opinion, for what it's worth.'

He looked pleased to be asked, though he always affected the plain dumb common-sense of the man-in-the-street.

'Marx was certainly right about one thing,' he went on, 'when he points out, for example, that the rising standard of living in mid-nineteenth century England rested largely on the miserable starvation wages paid to Indian labourers. But I can't see much sense in the rest of it. This man does not see *India* in his mind's eye. I can't get any feeling from him for the people, the landscape, the life. He reduces human beings to ciphers in a big theory. Marx thought that the older history of India, before the Raj, was contemptible. As far as I understand it, he thought India needed the Raj, to ripen the land into the capitalist mode of production, without which there could be no revolution of the people. So the Raj imposed a harsh discipline – a necessary pain – like a schoolmaster whipping a failing pupil. It didn't seem to matter if the schoolmaster was also vindictive and cruel.

'But that's all nonsense to me. I see this Marx as an authoritarian and a bully. A *mental* bully, trying to impose the authority of a theory, which may or may not have large elements of truth but had no place in it for the poor old Indian peasant. Now, I see the matter the other way round. I think that the Indian experience of the Raj was necessary to reform British imperialism, to temper the arrogance and stupidity of conquerors, and to teach us some democratic humility. All this wisdom, of course, came at a high cost to the Indians themselves.'

We were talking in a pub and it was my turn to get the beer. When I returned my father had a distant look in his eye. He was ready to sum up.

'I took one big lesson from all my years in India,' he continued. 'It seemed to me that the Raj, taken overall, was infatuated with India, as well it might be, considering the wealth of the culture, the wonderful variety of the people, and the contribution to world history. For me, and I was not untypical, India was one long love affair. Unhappily, as in most affairs of the heart, we members of the Raj botched it. The relationship went sour. We lacked sympathy and understanding. You may say that the Indians also had their faults. True enough. But it is not the job of a subject people to remedy the defects of the masters. We wanted too much and gave too little, not in terms of administration or politics or economics where, I think, we did quite well, but in our paucity of imagination, our stuffy emotions and lack of heart. Another case, I'm afraid, of British constipation.'

I was surprised that my father, a reticent man, had let himself go to this extent. Yes, I thought, in India we were lucky, very lucky. We were dealing with peoples and cultures that let us off easily. They preferred to expend their venom on each other. We came out with relatively clean hands (in so far as a greedy and selfish empire can ever be said to have clean hands). I think they saw us as lame cases who needed a helping hand. Or were we rescued just by intelligent good humour? They saw our difficulties and limitations and it amused them to play along. I recalled a tale told by an Indian writer about Govind Pant, the Chief Minister of United Provinces. Pant, as a young lawyer, was returning to his village dressed in Indian clothes:

'I met an English subaltern as I got out of the bus,' Pant related the story to Prem Bhatia. 'Seeing me dressed in Indian clothes he asked me to carry his bags. "You didn't do that!" Yes, said Pant, and at the end of the job he gave me two annas. "Why did you do it?" Don't get upset, he said, I did it deliberately to prepare myself to throw the British out. Let me see how far they will go to humiliate us. The subaltern was a stupid young man – I didn't mind.'

Perhaps, in the final analysis, empires are stupid too. Just wait, and they will fall apart.

★

There was much to be done. We were leaving, so far as we knew for ever. Wooden crates for furniture were ordered, new trunks bought, stencils of addresses cut, household goods sorted and set aside, ready to be packed for early despatch. My mother and the servants were busy, but without enthusiasm.

My mother was weeding out old clothes, holding garments up to the light, dithering over socks and shirts. Take them or leave them? What did it matter? Suddenly serviceable summer clothes were thrown on the discard pile. The flimsy clothes of India were no use now. England meant drizzles, cold winds, chilblains. Then she would hurry from the room, distracted, the job half done. 'There you are,' she would mumble as we passed in the door. 'Just leave those things, I'll come back to them. Now where was I?'

In the dismantling of the household my father was little help. External arrangements for passage and transportation were made through military offices. It was enough for him that he kept an eye on this bureaucracy. In the house, he did not care what stayed and what went. My mother had always chosen the household goods – the rattan furniture, the lamps decorated with the Aryan swastika that the Nazis later appropriated (in Sanskrit it means 'well-being'), the stiff Indian carpets of factory manufacture and doubtful quality, the little felt numdahs, the Benares brassware, the dull wooden carvings, the vases and the knick-knacks. My father's domestic needs were slight: a comfortable chair, a well-placed lamp, a pile of books, a large ashtray, a modest store of beer. He ate what was put in front of him (so long as it was not too fancy), murmuring invariably, 'yes, very nice, very nice,' in an abstracted voice. Then sometimes he looked down at his plate in surprise, wondering what he had eaten and if it *had* been very nice. He slept wherever a bed was placed and made ready, hurrying into oblivion for as many hours as he could manage.

The servants were touchy and despondent. A stern word to the houseboy sent him away snivelling. Even the older ones looked lost. They had worked hard to fit themselves for the service of the Raj, and for the best ones that service was not just a job but a calling, a vocation, often running in the family. It demanded tact, judgement, charm, a body of alien knowledge (the proper ranking of guests, the correct fork for fish, the right temperature for red wine, the order of the medals pinned on a dress uniform), skill with a foreign language (English), honesty in a land where the little criminalities of bribes, baksheesh and back-handers were not unknown. Now these servants were about to be abandoned. Even the old hands went about with their heads down, not so much sulking but with the accusatory look of loyal followers who had been deceived.

In these days I lost sight of Rahul, our pal, the bearer's son. Was he lying low out of misery? Had he been sent back to the family village in the Western Ghats? Or was he merely hidden away, redoubling his effort for the exams that were now likely to be more important then ever to him and his family? He was the hope for the future.

I did not ask where he was because, after all, he was only the son of a servant, and I was the young sahib who had not yet learnt how to behave to a human, my fellow, my Indian brother.

★

Preparing for our departure we no longer went to school. Everyone was too busy to mind about us. We mooched about the house and compound, getting in the way. Our bicycles were gone – given away, I think, for they were strange machines of no value, cobbled together from many different parts – and we could no longer ride to the swimming-pool in Secunderabad where our school friends went. But we still, occasionally, had the use of the divisional general's private pool in Bolarum.

The monsoon had passed leaving a season of mild warmth. For some, it was even too cool to swim. But the rainy days had left all waters swollen and fresh. Just to smell it was invigorating. The small pool belonging to the general was in a slight bowl of the ground, cut off from the house by a thick belt of bushes and trees, many of which, in this season of growth, crowded down on the concrete margin of the pool and overhung the water. A diving-board with frayed coconut matting projected from a steep bank at the deep end. From the board, giving a tentative spring or two, I looked down on the small green solitude of the water, the surface dull, dark, ominous under shadow, hardly reached by the sun except briefly around noon. No one else seemed to use the pool, at least not while we were there. The silence spread over us, as thick as the shade.

Suddenly taking courage in hand I dived into a hidden depth, flinging myself off the board in an act of faith.

★

By the side of the house, in the shade of big trees, Sami the bearer was painting stencilled addresses on the crates while my father was supervising him. They thought they were alone, though I could hear them clearly through the open window of our bathroom where I was enthroned on the thunderbox.

'Colonel sahib,' Sami said in a low voice, 'can you take me with you to England?'

'No, Sami,' replied my unemotional father almost tenderly, 'what would you do there?'

'I don't know. Perhaps I could work for you. You could help me, you are my father.'

'Unfortunately, it's not that easy. There are rules, you know. And you have your family. Times are difficult in England now, after the war. I don't know what I could do for you. Besides, my own future is uncertain. It would be wrong of me to tell you to go to England and then to find that you were unhappy or without a job and that I could not help you.'

'Yes, Colonel sahib. Thank you, thank you.'

I peeked cautiously out of the window. Sami was immediately at work painting the stencils again. My father was smoking, seated on the corner of a crate. I do not know who looked the more sad.

*

At Christmas, my parents gave me a box containing a tin fort that had to be assembled in a complicated way, with slits and tabs that were hard to align. I was a difficult boy to please with presents, having no interest in toys and little in books, preferring to spend my time and energy on outdoor adventure. When I had put the fort together, with some ill humour, I saw that it was modelled on a Hollywood version of a Foreign Legion fort. It had sand–coloured walls manned by cut-out figures of soldiers in kepis with ancient, long–barrelled rifles. A tin French flag waved from the battlements. I think there was a camel or two in the background. With surly ingratitude I did not want this fort, finding it anachronistic and unreal, and in the circumstances painful to contemplate. It had nothing to do with the pressing moment of departure. It was also a reminder of sun and soldiers and the vastness of open land under permissive skies where almost nothing was forbidden the privilege of boyhood.

When we left I managed to forget it, hiding it behind paper and rubbish at the bottom of a cupboard.

Early in January 1948 we left Bolarum for the journey north and west to the transit camp at Deolali where we waited to go to Bombay for the passage back to England. The camp was unpleasant, crowded and ugly, with rain-stained walls and tin roofs. It was a sluice through which India was being emptied of white faces, and time was too short for the maintenance and improvements that the

camp needed. Besides, these were heart-stopping days in India, with
the whole of the north in the tumult of partition. Five million
people were uprooted, wanderers, looking for home. For us, there
was no great hardship. The transients of the Raj endured a little
discomfort, ordering their memories, more fearful of the future than
the present.

We had booked our passage on the *Empress of Scotland*, due to
leave Bombay on Sunday, 1 February. We would make the short
train journey to Bombay on the day before the ship sailed.

In the early evening of Friday, 30 January, a Hindu named
Nathuram Godse, a skinny figure in khaki bush jacket and blue
trousers, approached Mahatma Gandhi as the venerable leader
walked from Birla House in New Delhi to the evening prayer
meeting on the lawn. At a distance of about five feet Godse greeted
Gandhi with the customary Hindu salutation – the raised hands
joined together in the *namaste*. Gandhi, leaning as usual on the
shoulders of his two grand-nieces, smiled and said a word or two,
preparing to return the salutation. At that point Godse pulled a .38
Beretta from his pocket and fired three times, at a range too close to
miss. Gandhi was hit in the chest, stomach and groin. He fell with
his hands at head level, joined together in the *namaste*. He was
carried into Birla House and died within half an hour, at about
5.40 p.m.

Next day, as we had arranged, we travelled by train to Bombay.
Something had happened, to be sure, but as a young boy I was not
aware of the grotesque enormity of the event. But all the adults
made that train journey with heart in mouth. What appalling
conflagration of ethnic and religious hatred might be waiting in
Bombay, that ever-volatile city? In Bombay there was trouble and
grief and mourning. But it was the stunned murmur of shock rather
than the violent outpouring of rage, for the simple and telling fact
was that the murder had been committed by a Hindu fanatic and not
by a Muslim.

What could my parents feel except emptiness? The substance of
their lives – all that brave commitment to a foreign land, that hope
and expectation, that activity and adventure, that *fun* – all narrowed
down meanly to a miserable retreat, glancing fearfully over the

shoulder lest death was following. I too was in the grip of something insupportable. I could not put a name to it. Grouchy and fretful I left with ill grace, feeling privately in the core of my being that India had failed me.

★

In later years, thinking about these events and trying to place them more justly in the history and the culture of the land, I concluded that India had two main effects on its conquerors and settlers: the power to disappoint, and the power to catch hold of the heart.

No one has expressed the sense of disappointment in India better than the Emperor Babur in the 1520s, and because of the charm of his personality and the keenness of his eye he is worth quoting.

'Hindustan is a country,' he wrote in his *Memoirs*,

> that has few pleasures to recommend it. The people are not handsome. They have no idea of the charms of friendly society, of frankly mixing together, or of familiar intercourse. They have no genius, no comprehension of mind, no politeness of manner, no kindness or fellow-feeling, no ingenuity or mechanical invention in planning or executing their handicrafts, no skill or knowledge in design or architecture; they have no horses, no good flesh, no grapes or musk-melons, no good fruits, no ice or cold water, no good food or bread in their bazaars, no baths or colleges, no candles nor torches, not a candlestick.

Warming to his indictment he lets loose some further salvoes.

> Except the rivers and streams that flow in their ravines and hollows, they have no running water of any kind in their gardens or palaces. In their buildings they study neither elegance nor climate, appearance nor regularity. Their peasants and the lower classes all go about naked. They tie on a thing which they call a *langoti*, which is a piece of clout that hangs down two spans from the navel, as a cover to their nakedness.

So there you have it, and what would you expect in the land of such a people?

The country and towns of Hindustan are extremely ugly. All the towns and lands have a uniform look. In many places the plain is covered by a thorny brushwood, to such an extent that the people of the pergannas, relying on these forests, take shelter in them, and often continue in a state of revolt, refusing to pay their taxes. In Hindustan, the populousness and decay, or total destruction of villages, nay of cities, is almost instantaneous.

To underline this dismal catalogue of a hopeless and dreary state, the emperor's translators and editors, sound Indiamen of the Raj, added a sage footnote: 'Babur's opinions regarding India are nearly the same as most Europeans of the upper class, even at the present day.'

But why did Babur not leave, this brilliant and effervescent Turkic chieftain, passionate about war and dominion but more passionate about life and love and the understanding of man? Towards the end of his life something strange happened. The truth is he could not escape India, and in the end he too became Indian.

It is a moving story. As his son and heir lay dangerously ill at Agra, Babur hurried to Humayun's bedside. He saw clearly that only his own sacrifice could save his son. Three times Babur walked around the sick-bed, saying, 'I take upon myself all that you suffer.' From that moment Humayun began to recover, and Babur declined to an early death at the age of forty-seven.

At last, India had caught him and taught him the great lesson of her history: to accept all, to forgive all, and to be resigned to the fate of all.

★

On the appointed day, undisturbed by riots, our ship left Bombay for the long trudge home on stormy seas. The war was over but the *Empress of Scotland* was still a troop-ship and delivered all the well-known discomforts of its kind. My brother and I were put in a long narrow cabin not far above the waterline. It had a single blurred porthole and a double tier of bunks down one long side. There were six of us in the cabin, two boys and four fairly senior officers ranked major and above.

The passage was rough. The ship bucked and thumped, the

groaning plates seeming to echo to the drowned ghosts of the sea. A
seasick major lay supine in a top bunk, too giddy to crawl into the
air. I, too, was seasick, retching misery into a yellowing toilet bowl
until I could heave no more. After a time the storms eased and the
motion altered from short-pitched plunges of startling ferocity to a
long easy wallow.

One morning, when I was at last able to stand in line in crumpled
pyjamas, waiting to clean my teeth at the single basin, a colonel of
unforgiving cheeriness, who admitted that he felt let down if he had
not experienced 'a good blow' at sea, saw me watching him at the
basin. He spooned white powder into a glass and formed a fizzy
cascade of bubbles.

'Hallo, young man,' he beamed at me. 'Feeling better now? Take
my advice and start the day with Andrew's Liver Salts. That's just the
ticket to get you going. You try it every day and you'll see you can't
go wrong.'

Then in some profound sense I knew I was heading 'home'. Good
citizenship and self-reliance were based on the superior action of the
liver and bowels. India was a chapter I had closed. The ship went
slowly on, pitching and grumbling as the wind picked up again. I
was ready to be sick once more, Liverpool-bound.

EPILOGUE

Where Am I Now?

ABOUT THIRTY YEARS after I left India, in a disordered time of life, with decisions not taken and commitments unclear, I was tempted by two friends to go with them on a winter journey to the south of Spain. One friend had the use of a small bleak village house in the mountains of Andalucia; the other friend had the impressive but unreliable BMW car to get us there.

Some journeys are well-planned, others tempt fate. Ours was of the second kind. Three restless spirits, chafing against the time, set out at a whim. Within half an hour of departing, one December morning, the car broke down. We spent the best part of the day in and about a pub in the suburbs of South London. The place, on that chill morning, had a hopeless air of indifference and hard-bitten use. Two of us – the unmechanical ones – stared into long glasses of unpleasant beer, watching a barman spread grime over the floor with a filthy mop. Outside, in the alleyway, our car-owner and practical mechanic lay in the gutter putting a kind of jury-rig on the suspension of the BMW.

In late afternoon, way behind schedule, we dashed for the Channel port. The night-ferry from Newhaven, almost empty of vehicles and passengers, had the desolation of a mausoleum, a doomed space sweating with the cold salty drip of the sea. The cafeteria was closed, there was no hot water, the vinyl-covered benches on which we tried to rest were dank with clammy condensation. In the French night the weather was raw and blustery. Claps of wind and sudden dark posses of rain pursued us down long avenues of poplars and pollarded limes. The car was uneasy to drive, fidgeting across the rumbles of the road. Two of us shared the

driving, and the non-driver – an Irishman – made it his business to
keep us awake. Tatters of wind-lashed cloud raced across a waning
moon. The Irishman, lolling at ease in the back seat, regaled us with
descriptions of stupendous meals, luscious dishes, gourmet feasts,
august wines, whose names are only mentioned in whispers, drawn
from subterranean cellars of eccentric oenophiles. We had not eaten
for almost twenty-four hours. Even the saliva in my mouth had
dried up.

Across France we hardly stopped, except for petrol and the slim
makings of a picnic that we ate on the run. By the time we reached
the Spanish border we were ravenous. At a truck stop, high in the
Basque country, where the parking-lot was packed with the mud-
stained lorries of professional truckers, we watched sombre men
with brawny forearms, the knobby faces of gluttons and bellies like
drums tear into mighty portions of meat or seafood washed down
with many carafes of coarse red wine. Then they launched their rigs
down mountain roads, trailers swinging across the centre line, and
we followed gingerly, now sober and awake.

A wide landscape, with dwindling traffic, the engine-beat of the
car steady and soporific. We fled south over the stubbled prairie of
Castile. In our car the drivers were growing weary, washed out,
lapsing into silence. The Irishman in the back had run out of stories.
No more fun. Towards the end of the night we reached Madrid,
plunging into a long tangle of city streets from which there seemed
to be no escape. We had neglected to provide ourselves with a city
map. A new system of relief roads had just been completed but was
as yet without road-signs. There was no one to ask in the dead
winter night. Guessing our way we navigated past the same hulking,
moon-splashed church three times before we punched clear from
the web of the city.

Beyond the suburbs finally, in a huddle of roadside shacks, we saw
a weak light in an early labourers' bar and stopped for coffee and
quick shots of anis seco. Outside, two patient mules snuffled at hay
and scraped pensive hoofs on the gravel of the lay-by.

It was my turn to drive. The sun was struggling up, looking
smudged and watery but for us the life-giving star that rescued us
from night. The road ran straight south, like a thin scar across the full

abdomen of Spain. The two passengers, hunched in awkward shapes, were at last rocked into sleep. I too was tired. The unvarying line of the road dragged at my eyelids. The murmur of the engine and the quiet drumming of the tyres made a lullaby. My head dropped, then shot up again with a monstrous charge of adrenalin jolting through my body. For a few seconds I had drifted into sleep and the car had slipped down the slight camber of the road into the wide, shallow ditch on the right. At 50 mph we jarred into the bottom of the ditch, bouncing over stones and rough ground, and then I was fully conscious again, wrestling the bucking steering-wheel to pull us back onto the road. In this hectic moment I over-compensated. The car spurted out of the dirt, a back wheel spinning, then gripped and dashed at an angle across the tarmac onto the wrong side of the road. In a second or two I regained control and had it straight, but when I looked up I saw, directly in my pathway at a distance of about two hundred yards, a big Pegaso truck charging upon us. I flicked the wheel to the right and accelerated. I saw the truck-driver in the high cab, his face a rictus of panic, standing on the brakes. Then the mudguard of the truck seemed to pass over our left shoulder and the truck went by with a roar of engine and a blast of air-horn that sounded like a dam breaking. In a few seconds we were clear and alone in an empty winter morning.

As soon as I could pull off onto level ground I stopped and we all climbed out warily, leaving the doors open. The car-owner had some solicitous looks for his vehicle, then swung himself under the chassis to check for damage. The Irishman, looking bemused, was about to say something but thought better of it and lit a cigarette. I walked apart to urinate. Then I got into the back seat and lay down and we drove off without a word. I dozed for some time, only becoming fully awake when we stopped on the apron of a sharp new roadside restaurant, all blue-patterned tiles and Moorish arches and a long sloping red roof. Peeping in we saw it was closed and deserted, so we strolled in the mild sunlight and someone tried a joke about our memory of momentary horror.

Ahead, a broken line of hills, like a faint wash on a watercolour was just visible, and somewhere beyond that were the pewter seas of the Mediterranean. We gazed that way and I think the same thought was in each of our minds: 'Despite bad omens the gods are with us so far. Fingers crossed that we get to the sea.'

★

We got there, of course. In the hill village it was cold, the wind snapping suddenly round the corners of steep cobbled streets. I felt the lassitude that comes after bad times and danger. My companions were stiff from the long cramps of the ride and chilled from weather and after-shock. In those December days the village closed early, battened into darkness soon after the Angelus bell, with only a few lights and an open bar by the main square. Reluctant to face the empty, unheated house too soon we went to the Bar Espejo for a dish of tough chicken and stayed there within reach of the butano heater ordering rounds of ciento-tres, Malaga dulce, raw local wine and stuff that was even worse. We talked of this and that, with long silences, but no one cared to mention the whiff of death that we had caught that morning. At about eleven we stumbled up the rough black street, a little bit drunk, and went to bed in a house of bitter discomfort and almost no furniture. I had a sleeping-bag spread on a floor of sloping flagstones.

Next morning, I found the Irishman pacing the kitchen, stroking his beard.

'How you feeling?' he said, giving me a leery look.

'OK,' I replied, 'all things considered.'

'Weird night, what?'

'Was it? I slept pretty well.'

'No funny stuff, then?'

'What do you mean?'

'Let me tell you a story,' he said, pouring hot water over grains of instant coffee.

He had woken suddenly in the night, jerked from sleep by the sense of someone prowling in the room. In the poor light he had seen a figure and after a few moments had recognized it as me. He was about to speak to me when something in the obsessive shuffling steps made him stop. The motions were those of dreams, and then it came to the Irishman that I was sleepwalking. Face to the wall I began to rearrange some shoes lined up on the floor, pushing them about like toy boats in a child's bath. And all the time I was talking, low-pitched words that had the stamp of coherence and organization. The sound of this language seemed oddly familiar, and in a while he had placed it. It was the sound of an Indian tongue, such as he had heard among the Indians of the newsagents and small grocery shops in his part of North London. Afraid to wake me, the Irishman sat up in bed wondering what to do. After a while I abandoned the shoes and sidled out of the bedroom, closing the door carefully behind me.

Awake and conscious, I have now no memory of Hindi, apart from a few mispronounced numbers and some broken sentences of the kind that the Raj would address to servants. All my conscious effort, in fact, has been given to another linguistic task, to try to get on good terms with English, a process I expect to last the rest of my life.

So I conclude that the 'I' of my waking mind is somehow less than the whole person. Like icebergs, we are supported by a hidden subliminal level which, again like icebergs, may be weightier than all that's seen.

I am more than I know myself to be. Out of my childhood emerges a cloaked figure, Western genes grafted to Indian environment. We pull back the cloak. Light falls on the whole person, a completed and manifest history. I rub my eyes in astonishment: I wonder, where am I now?